SAGA *of the* PILGRIMS

SAGA

of the

PILGRIMS

From Europe to the New World

by JOHN HARRIS

The
Globe
Pequot
press

CHESTER, CONNECTICUT

Cover Art

Samoset Bids the Pilgrims Welcome at Plymouth, 1621, by Charles Hoffbauer; photograph by William Ryerson, reprinted courtesy of *The Boston Globe;* reproduced by permission of The New England, Boston, Massachusetts.

Departure of the Pilgrims from Delfthaven in the Speedwell, by W. van de Velde; photograph by William Ryerson, reprinted courtesy of *The Boston Globe;* reproduced by permission of the Pilgrim Hall Museum, Plymouth, Massachusetts.

Text art credits appear on page 107.

Library of Congress Cataloging-in-Publication Data

Harris, John, 1908-
    Saga of the Pilgrims: From Europe to the New World/by John Harris. —1st ed.
        p.   cm.
    Includes index.
    ISBN 0-87106-462-6
    1. Pilgrims (New Plymouth colony) 2. Massachusetts—History—New
Plymouth, 1620–1691. I. Title.
F68.H276 1989
974.4'02—dc20   89-34786
                                                                 CIP

Manufactured in the United States of America
First Edition/First Printing

TABLE *of* CONTENTS

ACKNOWLEDGMENT *and* THANKS

In preparing text and locating illustrations I have had the generous help of many individuals. To all I most cordially express my thanks, especially to the following:

In England: Rev. Edmund F. Jessup, All Saints Church, Babworth; M. E. Bishow, Lord Chamberlain's Office, London; Verger Norman Ash, St. Andrew's Church, Plymouth; Rev. Nicholas Richards, St. Mary's Church, Rotherhithe; Sheila D. Thomson, City Archives, Southampton.

In Holland: Dr. Jeremy D. Bangs, Pilgrim Fathers Documentatie Centrum, Leyden.

In the United States: William Ryerson, *Boston Globe* photographer; Rodney Armstrong, Jack Jackson, Sally Pierce, Boston Athenaeum; Thomas W. Parker, Mary Leen, Bostonian Society; Sinclair Hitchings, Helen Sevagian, Kathleen B. Hegarty, Boston Public Library; Mary McLellan, State Library, and Albert Whittaker, State Archives, both at the State House, Boston; Louis Tucker, Winifred Collins, Massachusetts Historical Society; Harley P. Holden, Archives, and William H. Bond, Houghton Library, both at Harvard University; Sumner A. Webber, Coopers Mills, Maine, and Anthony J. Douin, Augusta, Maine; Lawrence Pizer, Caroline Chapin, Jeanne Mills, Pilgrim Hall, Plymouth, Mass.; James Baker, Rosemary Carroll, Plimoth Plantation, Plymouth, Mass.; Chester Peck, Pilgrim Monument Museum, Provincetown, Mass.; Dorothy Wentworth, Duxbury, Mass.

—JOHN HARRIS

SAGA
of the
PILGRIMS

Arrested While Trying to Flee

"There was a large company of them purposed to get passage at Boston in Lincolnshire, and for that end had hired a ship wholly to themselves and made agreement with the master to be ready at a certain day. . . ."

An eyewitness and participant, William Bradford, then seventeen years of age, described in those words the beginning of the Pilgrims' first heart-breaking attempted migration from the English Midlands that would eventually lead—by chance—to the first permanent colonization in a faraway land, later called New England.

The time: mid-autumn, 1607.

Why had these people, these farmers—Bradford said that they "had only been used to a plain country life and the innocent trade of husbandry"—engaged a shipmaster to take them out of the land beloved alike among generations of their ancestors and themselves? Why? Because they were being persecuted by their new sovereign, James I, recently arrived from his kingdom, Scotland.

King James, like his predecessor, Elizabeth I, was an absolute monarch, combining in his crown and person control over church and state. Soon after arriving from Scotland, he proclaimed before the highest civil and ecclesiastical British authorities, gathered at his Hampton Court palace, west of London, that he would make all his subjects conform to his state religion or hound any dissenters out of his realm.

In dismissing the Puritan clergy's appeal to end abuses, King James, who believed that he ruled by "divine right," proclaimed: "I will have one doctrine and one discipline, one religion in substance and ceremony. . . . I shall make them conform themselves, or I will harry them out of the land or else do worse. If any would not be quiet, and show his obedience, he were worthy to be hanged."

The king, a pedantic character who fancied his own pompous commentaries on matters of religious dispute, did accede to one Puritan request, the preparation of a new translation of the Bible. This, in tribute to the royal permission, would be called the King James Bible, for which scholars labored until 1611—several years after the Pilgrims started to flee from England.

"There was no hope," said Bradford, that these people, about to become self-exiles, could stay in their remote Midland area, the village of Scrooby and its surrounding hamlets at the northern tip of Nottinghamshire where it borders closely on Yorkshire to the north and Lincolnshire to the east. Moreover, said Bradford, they had heard that in Holland, across the North Sea from Boston in Lincolnshire, they could enjoy a hope denied to them in England: "Freedom of religion for all men."

Years would pass before these English husbandmen and their wives and children would become known as Pilgrims. To the authorities they were known as something worse than dissenters. They were separatists—people eschewing the state church altogether despite brutal penalties that might be imposed upon them. Brownists: that was the name by which they were known, a name critics conceived in derision thinking of Rev. Robert Browne, prominent separatist in the 1580s.

Daily life in Scrooby had been drained of sweetness for them after James I acceded to the British throne.

"They were scoffed and scorned by the profane multitude," said Bradford, when it became known that they believed they should make their own covenant with God, should reject the "courts, canons and ceremonies" of the state church, and should try to live a simple Biblical life, as in the time of Christ and His Apostles.

Bradford, writing about the "profane multitude" referred to nationwide reaction to nonconformists. Still, Puritans had been steadily increasing in England, though the very name Puritan was originally devised by their maligners "to cast contempt." Puritans did desire to remain with the state church, but sought to purify its practices in ways described in the New Testament.

The Pilgrims likewise were Puritans. But they were extreme Puritans, feeling that they could pursue a Biblical life only by separating from the state church. These Brownists of Scrooby were comparatively few.

Clergymen whose consciences drew them toward nonconformity all over England were being forced by their bishops to take oaths of uniformity or be silenced and deprived of their religious posts.

"And poor people were so vexed with apparitors and pursuivants [officers enforcing conformity] and commissary [church] courts, as truly their affliction was not small. Which, notwithstanding, they bore sundry years with much patience."

Early Brownists, in Queen Elizabeth's day, had seen many of their clergy hanged—martyred for their conscientious refusal to conform. For the Scrooby Brownists the truly perilous times came, about a year before they resolved to emigrate, when they began "exercising the worship of God amongst themselves, notwithstanding all the diligence and malice of their adversaries. . . ."

Bradford told how "they could not long

Arrows show Pilgrims' escape routes, first to an area near Boston, England, and later to Immingham Creek.

continue in any peaceable condition, but were hunted and persecuted on every side, so as their former afflictions were but as flea-bitings in comparison of those which now came upon them.

"For some were taken and clapped up in prison, others had their houses beset and watched night and day, and hardly escaped their hands; and the most were fain to flee and leave their houses and habitations, and the means of their livelihood."

With these Brownists, serving as their chosen pastor and teacher, were two clergymen whose nonconformity had deprived them of their livings. One was Rev. Richard Clyfton, from the neighboring hamlet of Babworth. The other was Rev. John Robinson, from Norwich, center of Puritanism in East Anglia, an area from which later emigrated many of the first settlers in the future Massachusetts Bay colony, bringing with them shire names: Norfolk, Essex, and Suffolk.

For the Scrooby Brownists the worst threatened disaster was that punitive legal action had been set in motion against their mainstay, the man most responsible for their religious inspiration and fellowship, the man Bradford said always made his purse cheerfully available, though "sometimes above his ability," the foremost citizen of Scrooby, William Brewster, who would become a preeminent founder of New England.

Like those of his father, Brewster's financial position and importance were solidly based on his being employed by the very highest authorities in the realm, the Archbishop of York and the Crown itself, Elizabeth I and then James I.

Brewsters had lived in this part of England for many generations. William Brewster, later renowned as the Pilgrims' revered ruling elder, probably was born in or near Scrooby in 1566. The customary parish records are simply not to be found. When

King James I required all his subjects either to conform to the state religion or leave the country.

Queen Elizabeth I sent many early Brownists to the gallows.

young William was nine years old his father, William senior, was given a signal, lucrative position.

Forty-five miles north of Scrooby was the seat of the Archbishop of York and York Cathedral. In 1575 the Archbishop of York, shortly to become Archbishop of Canterbury and thus Primate of England, referring to Brewster senior as "our trusted and well-beloved servant," made him his receiver and bailiff for life in Scrooby.

Brewster senior thus was provided the finest residence for miles around this rural farming country, Scrooby Manor, an occasional residence for the archbishop. Scrooby Manor had been part of the Archbishop of York's see since property records were first gathered in William the Conqueror's Domesday Book. The timber-and-brick manor house of Brewster senior's day, with all its thirty-nine rooms, fell into decay and later was all but demolished.

The manor house itself and its park were set on six or seven acres of land, enclosed by a moat. A great hall, the chapel, and the galleried main structure faced the slow-moving Ryton River. Beyond the moat and throughout Scrooby, with orchards and meadowlands, were the farms assigned to tenants and yeomen, some reedroofed, some thatched with straw. To these residents Brewster senior was rent gatherer and manorial magistrate.

Scrooby Manor had sheltered royalty on many resplendent occasions as far back as King John, who signed the Magna Charta at Runnymede in 1215.

Princess Margaret, sister of Henry VIII, spent a night at Scrooby Manor on her way to Scotland to marry its Stuart king, a marriage from which devolved the rights of her grandson, James I, to the throne of England. Henry VIII himself, like his royal father, had sojourned at Scrooby Manor, and we can fancy the pageantry and local excitement as the

Brewster and the Pilgrims frequently gathered at Scrooby Manor (much altered since Brewster's time).

The other source of Brewster senior's ample income was the Great North Road that ran some 350 miles from London to Edinburgh, capital of Scotland. This main road, which now passes to the westward, in Brewster's time ran right through the village of Scrooby and here, 150 miles north of London, was the twelfth stage in the royal post to Scotland.

Brewster the elder was also the Scrooby postmaster.

In those days such a title involved duties far different from those of the modern postmaster. Brewster was a direct agent for the Crown and the Privy Council. Most of the messages forwarded were government dispatches. Brewster had to be prepared at all times to see royal couriers speedily—"within one quarter of an hour"—on their way, furnishing fresh horses, any needed "furniture," such as saddles, leather bags, or posthorns to be blown in passing "through any town or at least thrice every mile." Heavy penalties menaced any postmaster who failed in these duties.

They were furthermore to be prepared for official travelers' personal needs—shelter, food, and refreshment; to that end, the postmaster kept an inn in Scrooby Manor. Bradford pictures Brewster as a perfect host: "wise and discreet and well-spoken," also "of a very cheerful spirit, very sociable and pleasant. . . ."

cavalcade with lords, knights, and retainers accompanied these royal progresses and filled to overflowing the great manorial hall and rooms.

Cardinal Wolsey, Henry VIII's great Lord Chancellor and former Archbishop of York, sought comfortable safety here, temporarily avoiding the monarch's towering rage that led to Wolsey's downfall.

Just a short distance south of Scrooby is Sherwood Forest—then heavily wooded—the fabled haunt for Robin Hood and his Merry Men. Queen Elizabeth, who traveled constantly about her realm, was so charmed by Scrooby Manor as to request it for her own, but the archbishop pleaded his need for its revenues and the queen acceded.

James I, a frequent and tireless hunter, thought Scrooby Manor a fine lodge for him when chasing game in Sherwood Forest. En route from Scotland to London in 1603 to assume the throne, James "sat down on a bankside to eat and drink" by the Ryton River. While at his royal picnic the king must have been told about nearby Scrooby Manor, for he soon said to the Archbishop of York that though Scrooby Manor was "exceedingly decayed" it would provide him with an abode when he wished "to take our pleasure" in Sherwood Forest.

But once again the archbishop weathered the royal whim and retained the manor. And so too did the Brewsters.

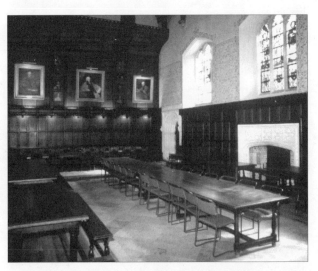

Brewster ate meals at this buttery while he was attending Peterhouse College at Cambridge University.

This employment by Crown and archbishop brought the Brewsters substantial advantages. Young Brewster when fifteen years of age traveled south through Sherwood Forest to the University of Cambridge, about 100 miles away, and entered Peterhouse College. He was a pensioner, which meant he could afford to pay for his lodgings, keep, and education.

Cambridge in 1580 was already the main center for British nonconformist, Puritan thinking, and among the men then at the university a number would be imprisoned, exiled, or martyred on the scaffold for following their religious convictions. Young Brewster, a studious, serious youth, learned to speak in Latin and had insight "in ye Greek." At Peterhouse, Bible clerks read Scripture aloud during meals.

Mary Queen of Scots was executed on orders of Queen Elizabeth for allegedly aiding Spanish plans to invade England.

Like many sons of the gentry, Brewster left the university before graduation, his economic future like theirs being secure. Brewster left in 1583 for the center of the realm, London, to join the staff and household of a man who would shortly be among the highest officials in England, William Davison. Bradford called Davison "religious and godly"; he was a skilled diplomat, one of the best serving the ever-devious Queen, and he was also a Puritan.

Davison handled the most important missions, traveling to Scotland to block its alliance with France and going often to the Low Countries in Queen Elizabeth's on-again, off-again efforts to help the Dutch in their long, uphill war of liberation from Spain. Davison, Bradford relates, came to esteem young Brewster rather "as a son than a servant." This father-and-son relationship would develop years later between Brewster and the twenty-four-year-younger, orphaned William Bradford.

On emergency mission to Holland in 1586, after Spain had overwhelmed the Low Country stronghold at Antwerp, imperiling the Dutch cities to the north, Davison went to Leyden to provide the Dutch with an English army. In return, the Dutch pawned three of their towns to pinchpenny Queen Elizabeth "as gages [security] for her expenses."

Brewster, then twenty years old, for the first time saw the community of Leyden, a few miles from The Hague. Leyden later would become the chief haven for the Pilgrims during most of their stay in Holland before their perilous voyage to the faraway New World. The town was already famed for withstanding a long Spanish siege and having, as a reward, the great Dutch liberator William the Silent establish there a celebrated university that would one day try to help the Pilgrims resist persecutions by James I.

So trusted was Brewster that Davison put in his care the keys to the three so-called cautionary Dutch towns in pledge to Queen Elizabeth. Brewster, said Bradford, slept with the keys "under his pillow." The Dutch, in tribute to Davison, presented to him a gold chain. While en route back to Dover and London to report to the queen, Davison had Brewster wear the gold chain "till they came to the Court."

Suddenly, after Davison's skills had elevated him to the Privy Council and the exalted office of Secretary of State, Davison's public career was wrecked by the queen's duplicity. He was made a scapegoat for the queen's ordering in 1587 that her second cousin, Mary Queen of Scots, Queen Elizabeth's closest blood relative, be beheaded.

Mary was imprisoned for nearly two decades, charged with treason in a plot to aid in a Spanish invasion of England and assassination of Queen Elizabeth. The queen had long hesitated about signing the death warrant, but when Lord Admiral Howard, who would command the British ships a year later against the Spanish Armada, urged her to do so, the queen told Davison to bring her the death warrant; she signed it.

Prior to that, Elizabeth had proposed that Davison arrange for Mary's jailer to poison Mary so that the queen could escape the obloquy for ordering Mary's execution. When the beheading had been carried out, Queen Elizabeth sent letters to Mary's son, then sitting on the Scottish throne as James VI. She told James, already in her pay, that the execution was a "lamentable accident . . . I had not so much as a thought of."

To support her royal pretense, Queen Elizabeth, lacing her words with her invariable rough oaths, ordered Davison imprisoned in the Tower of London. Her top adviser, Lord Burghley, and her favorite, handsome Lord Essex (a few years later she also ordered him beheaded) sought to save Davison. Essex said that "the Queen herself confesseth in her kingdom she has not such another." Inexorable Queen Elizabeth even had the Star Chamber impose on Davison a ruinous fine of 10,000 marks.

For slightly more than the two years while Davison was unjustly confined to the Tower, Brewster stayed close by, as Bradford said, doing the ailing Davison "many faithful offices of services in the times of his troubles."

St. Wilfred's Church still stands in Scrooby, appearing much as it did in Brewster's day.

When William Brewster senior became ill in 1589, his son returned to Scrooby Manor to assume his father's manorial and postal duties. A year later, the elder Brewster died.

In Scrooby, a short way from Scrooby Manor, still stands St. Wilfred's, the Anglican parish church, with its beautiful spire as in Brewster's day. He was a communicant and soon after his return to Scrooby he was married.

"He did much good in the country," said Bradford, "in promoting and furthering religion, not only by his practices and example . . . but by procuring good preachers to the places thereabout and drawing on of others to assist and help forward in such a work."

Brewster started introducing outside preachers to Scrooby and the neighboring hamlets—a widespread Puritan practice. The queen and her bishops were inflexibly set against preaching. Yet Brewster, said Bradford, for many years "walked according to the light he saw till the Lord revealed further to him." This was the revelation, Bradford intimated, which would come to Brownists that to remain in the state church would endanger their souls, and they must form a separate church.

That moment now came to Brewster. He was, said Bradford, "a special stay and help to them . . . after they were joined together in communion." These Brownists of Scrooby, these Pilgrims, made a covenant together, said Bradford, for Bradford, though hailing from Austerfield two and one-half miles north of Scrooby, was one of them.

"They ordinarily met at his [Brewster's] house on the Lord's Day, which was a manor of the Bishop's, and with great love he entertained them when they came, making provision for them to his great charge [expense], and continued to do so whilst they could stay in England. And when they came to remove out of the country he was one of the first in all adventures, and forwardest in any charge."

The gathering menace from the ecclesiastical court, already making arrests, was not the Pilgrims' only imminent danger.

On September 30, 1607, Brewster's postmastership was suddenly terminated when he resigned and a successor was named. The Crown had clearly become aware of Brewster's persistent nonconformist activities.

Escaping to Holland confronted the Pilgrims with difficulties that deeply troubled but did not dismay these resolute souls.

"Though they could not stay," said Bradford, "yet were they not suffered to go; but the ports and havens were shut against them, so as they were fain to seek secret means of conveyance, and to bribe and fee [pay] the mariners, and give extraordinary rates for their passages." Thus they joined the pathetic annals of mankind's inhumanity to refugees whose consciences forced them to differ.

King James would have them out of his kingdom. But to leave the kingdom required permits, and to seek permits meant self-incrimination. Penalties could be severe, and England then swarmed with spies and informers eager to turn in nonconformist neighbors and receive bounty from either the Bishop's High Court of Commission for Ecclesiastical Causes or the King's Privy Council.

Holland was still in a state of war with Spain. That condition aside, these religious refugees had another profound difficulty, told by Bradford:

"To go into a country they knew not but by hearsay, where they must learn a new language and get their livings they knew not how, it being a dear place and subject to the miseries of war, it was by many thought an adventure almost desperate, a case intolerable and a misery worse than death."

There is much about the flight from Scrooby we do not know.

Precisely when they left Scrooby; how many left (probably fewer than 100); how they got to the east-coast port of Boston, sixty-five miles southeast of Scrooby, Bradford left untold. Nor did he record which was that "certain day" on which they were to

meet the shipmaster and his ship, though he did say it was after dark.

"Brewster's giving up his postmastership may well have coincided with his completing arrangements for the ship to meet them at Boston. That "certain day" then would be in October. By then they would have had to dispose of all belongings save those which they could carry, keeping in mind that some were like Brewster's wife, Mary, who held in her arms their newborn child, their third, a girl strangely—or revealingly—named Fear.

They probably went as they had to their secret service in the chapel at Scrooby Manor, in small groups, inconspicuously, with no ringing of bells. Wheeled vehicles were uncommon in those days. The roads between villages were mostly little better than bridle paths, as were large stretches of even the Great North Road. To cross streams meant wading. Bridges were few in rural areas.

Thirty miles southeast of Scrooby, toward Boston, is the shire (county seat) town of Lincoln with its renowned cathedral, one of England's very largest, built by William the Conqueror. Had they boats, the Pilgrims could have gone from Lincoln down the Witham River to a remote creek below Boston, where they were to board their hired ship. Whether by boat or afoot they finally reached the creek on the Witham in flat fenland with great broad vistas of sky much like the Dutch coastland on the opposite side of the North Sea.

The surprise outcome of the Pilgrims' herculean attempt to flee has been recounted by Bradford. Recalling what the villainous English shipmaster did after subjecting them to "long waiting and large expenses," Bradford wrote:

"When he had them and their goods aboard, he betrayed them, having beforehand complotted with the searchers and other officers so to do, who took them, and put them into open boats, and there rifled and ransacked them, searching to their shirts for money, yea even the women further than became modesty, and then carried them back into the town and made them a spectacle and wonder to the multitude which came flocking on all sides to behold them."

After they had been "rifled and stripped of their money, books and much other goods" by the catchpoll officers (the sheriff's men who pursued debtors), they were presented to the local magistrates, and messengers were sent to London to inform the lords of the Privy Council. Then the Pilgrims "were committed to ward"; that is, they were placed under guard.

A few steps eastward from the Boston marketplace is the old Guild Hall with cells in the basement. These were insufficient for this "large company," and so most of the Pilgrims had to be placed in houses around the town.

A few steps from the opposite side of the marketplace, facing a bank of the river Witham, is St. Botolph's Church, one of the largest parish churches in England. Its 272-foot tower, "The Stump" to the natives, can be seen in these lowlands of England for miles around as well as from far out on the North Sea. At this remarkable church a few years later Rev. John Cotton carried out his Puritan labors until forced to flee to the New World, where he would become known as Patriarch of Massachusetts.

The spirit of Puritanism, already growing among the parishioners attending St. Botolph's Church, would be prodigiously helpful in the plight now confronting these unfortunate, betrayed Pilgrims.

Pilgrims were jailed at Guild Hall, near Boston marketplace, England.

St. Botolph's Church ("The Stump") was the center for Puritans who later settled in the New World's Boston.

Confronted with Stake and Scaffold

 citation before the Church Court of High Commission in December 1607 against William Brewster, while the Pilgrims were trying to flee to Holland, charged their leader with being "disobedient in matters of religion" and with being "a Brownist"—also known as Barrowist or Separatist.

How did it happen that such accusations arose in a remote, sparsely settled farming community in Midland England? And what terrifying background behind these charges would impel simple-living, peaceful farm people to break with their past and seek an uncertain future in a foreign land?

In later years, while Bradford instructed young Pilgrim men in America about the Pilgrims' religious background, he said that at the time the Pilgrims fled Scrooby they knew "certainly of six that were publicly executed besides such as died in prison."

Bradford meant the dreadful and tragic way in which the Brownist dissenters were treated in Queen Elizabeth's drive to enforce conformity.

The queen's instinctive aversion to all dissent makes it readily understandable that she, as supreme head of both church and state, would be angered by the Brownists' religious convictions. They believed the Bible taught that civil authority had no authority over religion. This was the incipient doctrine of separation between church and state, which for Queen Elizabeth constituted sedition tantamount to rebellion.

In the band of arrested Scrooby Pilgrims were two separatist clergymen: their pastor, Rev. Richard Clyfton, a man of about fifty-four, and their teacher, Rev. John Robinson, the future renowned "Pastor of the Pilgrims," then thirty-one. Clyfton, said Bradford in about his only physical description of a Pilgrim, was a "grave, and fatherly old man . . . having a great white beard."

The Brownist movement, in which these clergymen were pioneers, was the seedbed for the Congregational Church that later developed in early colonial New England. Its beginnings in England comprise what happened first in the London area and later in the Scrooby area to these extreme Puritans who espoused teachings by Rev. Robert Browne.

Rev. Browne was from a wealthy Midland family. His father, a knight, was related to Queen Elizabeth's closest adviser, Lord Burghley. Browne, trained at Cambridge, academic center of Puritanism, served as chaplain to the Duke of Norfolk, taught in Southwark, just across the River Thames south of London, and then spent more time at Cambridge in religious study.

Next, in 1580, Browne began his reformist ministry at Norwich, the Norfolk county shire town and center of intense Puritanism. In fact, Norwich, with its large population of Dutch who had fled to East Anglia to escape persecution by Spain's Philip II, was second only to London as a growing Puritan stronghold. Rev. Browne had been attracted to Norwich because he had heard that the people there were "very forward" in religion.

This choice did not spare him the bishop's official wrath. Rev. Browne was jailed a few times for nonconformity, and in 1582, thirty-two years old, he fled with his flock across the North Sea to tolerant and friendly Middleburg in Zealand, a part of Holland on the North Sea and nearest to England's East Anglia.

There he did something he had been unable to do in England. He published five books defining his faith and justifying separation from England's state church. "Magistrates," he postulated, "have no ecclesiastical authority." True Christians, he said, must separate themselves from a state church that fails to exclude the irreligious and, once separated, can achieve a "genuine and perfect church" when they "unite by a public covenant with each other and with God." Church authority, he maintained, rests on its members' interpretation of the Bible.

After two years in Zealand, Rev. Browne went off to Scotland when his flock fell apart over lack of church organization and parishioners' mutual criticisms. A few years later, on his return to England, Rev. Browne recanted, was readmitted to the state church, and was given a parish through Lord Burghley's efforts. The recantation was the reason being called a "Brownist" carried extra opprobrium.

Rev. Browne, after recanting, ceased to be a powerful figure in the pulpit. He had been confined in more than thirty prisons—loathsome, disease-ridden hellholes—and undoubtedly his once strong mind had been damaged in his long struggle for freedom of conscience. Still his recantation was far from the end of Brownism. The bishops soon provided Brownism with the ever-popular appeal of martyrs.

These martyrs included the six cited by Bradford whose public executions were so well known to the Pilgrims. Moreover, Brewster had even studied with some of these martyrs during his years at Cambridge University. And these, as Bradford recounted, were added to the many others who had lost their lives in the prisons in that harsh era.

That the Pilgrims were so keenly aware of the authorities' savage behavior strongly emphasizes the Pilgrims' unshakable resolution in ignoring threatened punishment and their persisting in preparation to flee England.

The first two martyrs were very plain folks just like the Pilgrims.

In the heart of East Anglia at Bury St.

The citation against Brewster by the Church Court

Edmunds, two men who had endured seven years off and on in prison for their nonconformity were charged with "dispersing of Browne's books" in England. They were humble men, a shoemaker named John Copping and a tailor named Elias Thacker. Seized Browne books were burned at the scaffold and Copping and Thacker were then hanged.

Their hanging, a double irony, was close by the old abbey of Bury St. Edmunds, in which the barons of England had drawn up their petition for freedoms that led to the Magna Charta.

The bishops did not get all Rev. Browne's books, but they did get the Star Chamber to buttress their control over printing and to establish, with still more dreadful penalties, regulations governing the licensing of press and printing. This capture helped to net two more nonconformists, the noted Henry Barrowe, a lawyer at London Grey's Inn, and the Rev. John Greenwood.

Barrowe was a familiar at Queen Elizabeth's court and had had a "libertine youth." Then, in 1586, possibly in his capacity as a lawyer, he visited Rev. Greenwood at the Clink Prison in Southwark, and was suddenly drawn to Greenwood's nonconformist teachings. The visit brought Barrowe's prompt arrest. Together in prison they discussed Rev. Browne's books. They took to putting their views on scraps of paper that were smuggled to Holland for printing.

Barrowe developed a new idea for establishing stability in church organization, an accomplishment that had eluded Rev. Browne in Zealand. Barrowe, saying that he found "sound proof . . . in Holy Scriptures," advocated that nonconformist church pastors be guided by elders. Barrowe did much more secret writing than Rev. Greenwood and may have had a part in preparing seven pamphlets, the first of which appeared in 1588 and titillated England, already bursting with exuberance, directly after the epochal victory over the Spanish Armada.

These were the seven "Martin Mar-prelate" pamphlets ridiculing the bishops for dishonesty and irreligion. The pamphlets made the bishops even more relentless in their efforts to control printing.

In Middleburg, Holland, at this time was Rev. Francis Johnson, another Cambridge University man like Rev. Browne, Barrowe, and Greenwood. Rev.

Johnson was pastor of the English Church in Middleburg where, to please the English ambassador, he helped to track down and burn some nonconformist treatises prepared in their London prison by Barrowe and Rev. Greenwood. Bradford tells how Rev. Johnson withheld two of these treatises from the flames so that he could peruse them.

Reading these treatises chastened and converted Rev. Johnson, whereupon he headed back across the North Sea to the Fleet Prison in London to visit Barrowe and Rev. Greenwood, once again jailed for holding illegal religious gatherings.

Presently London's Separatist Ancient Church in Southwark was formed, in 1592, with Rev. Johnson as pastor and Rev. Greenwood, momentarily free on bail, as teacher. Associated with him, with a price on his head, was one of William Brewster's classmates at Cambridge University, Rev. John Penry.

The authorities moved swiftly. Rev. Johnson and Rev. Greenwood were arrested by pursuivants while conducting services in the Fleet Street lodgings of a London haberdasher. And soon fifty-six members of the new church, while holding their religious service in the Islington Woods just north of the ancient London walls, were pounced on and thrown into London's stinking prisons: the Clink, Fleet, and Newgate.

The bishops proceeded to secure an even stronger law against nonconformists, "An act to retain the Queen's subjects in Obedience," aimed at the Brownists and Barrowists.

Anyone above sixteen years of age failing for a month to attend "the usual place of Common Prayer . . . to hear Divine Service" as established by her majesty's laws, or urging nonattendance by "printing, writing or speeches," could under this new law be imprisoned without bail until they conformed. If dissidents did not conform within three months they must leave the realm. If they should return, the law provided that they could be put to death "as in the case of felony, without benefit of clergy."

Barrowe and Rev. Greenwood were next brought into London's Old Bailey courtroom to answer new charges of sedition and, without even time for appeal, they were carted to Tyburn and hanged. A few weeks later Brewster's classmate, Rev. Penry, charged with printing derisive tracts, was executed on the gallows in Southwark. And in Norfolk still another nonconformist, little-known William Dennis of Thetford, was hanged.

These were the six "publicly executed" whom Bradford discussed in later years in the New World while relating the shocking perils the Pilgrims had to face. Bradford's nephew and secretary, Nathaniel Morton, in his preface to Bradford's remarks, said that the cause for which the six had perished "was in effect but what our church and the churches of Christ in New England do both profess and practice."

The number of believers who perished in contemporary ghastly prisons must certainly have been stupendous. Most of Rev. Johnson's flock did ultimately manage to escape to Holland's biggest community, Amsterdam. There in 1597, they were joined by Rev. Johnson after he had spent still more years in prison and had endured futile official efforts to deport him to the New World. Thus the martyr's Ancient Church of Southwark was renewed in Amsterdam.

Holland as a possible land of refuge and hope had been recurringly brought to the Pilgrims' notice. It was a land already known to the leader, Brewster, and successive condemnations of Separatist martyrs as the Scrooby congregation increased directed more and more Pilgrim attention to that country across the North Sea.

Like the Brownist leaders in London, Brewster and the clergymen involved in the Scrooby area had all been ousted or had resigned from their earlier parishes. Also all had received their training at Cambridge University and all, of course, had access to the illegally printed books by Barrowe and Rev. Browne.

Rev. Richard Clyfton, the parson with the great white beard, was the oldest. Thirteen years older than Brewster, he had become rector in the hamlet of Babworth, eight miles south of Scrooby, two years

Memorial commemorates martyrs and separatist leaders at Pilgrim Fathers' Memorial Church, Southwark, London.

before the Spanish Armada had struck. He was, said William Bradford, "a grave and reverend preacher, who, by his pains and diligence had done much good; and, under God, had been the means of the conversion of many."

Bradford knew at first hand, for Rev. Clyfton was his teacher. Bradford, as a teenager, had tramped more than ten miles partly along the Great North Road to listen to Rev. Clyfton preach. These trips were from Austerfield, a hamlet just north of Scrooby, where Bradford was born in 1590 into a prosperous, numerous family of husbandmen.

Bradford was only sixteen months old when his father died. His mother remarried, and then four-year-old Bradford was committed to his grandfather's care. By the time Bradford was seven his grandfather and mother were dead and Bradford's uncles, yeomen farmers, took over his care. Illness struck Bradford when he was eleven, keeping him from farm chores and leaving ample time for this natural scholar to read the Bible. Soon he was taking those long Sunday walks along the "Pilgrim Path"—from Scrooby to Babworth—to hear Rev. Clyfton.

The farming folk of Austerfield mostly attended their small, ancient Norman church of St. Helena—still to be seen—where Bradford was baptized. When Bradford became convinced that he should give up attendance at St. Helena's Church, he was faced with "the wrath of his uncles" and "the scoff of his neighbors now turned upon him as one of the Puritans. . . ." His response to them shows that Bradford shared in the resolution abundant among the early Pilgrims:

"I am not only willing to part with everything in this world for this cause, but I am also thankful that God hath given me a heart so to do; and will accept me so to suffer for him."

Bradford was baptized at St. Helena's Church, Austerfield.

In time, white-bearded Rev. Clyfton of Babworth became one of the "good preachers" Brewster invited to Scrooby Manor. When Rev. Clyfton gave up his rectorship at Babworth is uncertain, but he could well have been at the manor along with the orphaned Bradford, participating in services and discussions with his generous host Brewster. The time was before the Scrooby Pilgrims in fall 1606 "joined themselves by a covenant of the Lord . . . to walk in all His ways made known."

His own account, observed Bradford in later years, would show that this complete separation "cost them something." He meant not mere money but their patient suffering.

The other dismissed clergyman joining this Scrooby covenant, Rev. John Robinson, then about thirty years old, had begun his ministry near Norwich (where Rev. Browne had preached) in 1600. In 1604, after King James's devastating crackdown, Robinson's nonconformity was no longer endurable to his bishop and Robinson was dismissed. Indeed, a crushing consequence of the King's conference at Hampton Court was that some 300 clergymen all over England were deprived of their livings or felt compelled by conscience to quit their positions.

Rev. Robinson's wife came of a well-off family in a hamlet near Gainsborough, a large community on the River Trent in Lincolnshire, ten miles east of Scrooby. Rev. Robinson withdrew there from Norwich and pursued his religious study. This search for the truth, he said, was in his "heart as a burning fire shut up in my bones."

For a time, the Scrooby nonconformists walked to Gainsborough to hear the Rev. John Smyth preach in the hall of Gainsborough's ancient manor where King Henry VIII, after a stay at Scrooby Manor, once held his royal court.

Bradford, who often had heard Rev. Smyth, said that Rev. Smyth was a "man of able gifts and a good preacher."

While Rev. Smyth was at Cambridge University he had been tutored by Rev. Francis Johnson before Rev. Johnson's fiery reform preaching led to his being forced to leave the University. Rev. Smyth, after first preaching in Lincoln, had taken up his pastorate in Gainsborough. Plagued by religious doubts, Smyth had soon given up his pulpit in the state church and gathered the Separatist flock that worshipped in the old Gainsborough manor hall.

The "distance of place" from which Rev. Smyth's followers had to come for church services, said Bradford, led to the Gainsborough flock's splitting into "two distinct bodies." This division came in 1606 when the Scrooby Pilgrims decided to make their own covenant in Scrooby with Rev. Clyfton as their pastor and Rev. Robinson as their teacher.

Presently Rev. Smyth and the remainder of his flock fled from Gainsborough to Holland and formed the Second Exiled English Church in Amsterdam.

The Scrooby Pilgrims, with hope in England denied them, were next to try to flee to Holland.

Pilgrims are depicted leaving All Saints' Church, Babworth, to take the "Pilgrim Path" back to Scrooby.

From English Cells to Dutch Freedom

Bradford did not mention that the Boston magistrates' Puritan leanings aroused their compassion for the confined Pilgrim men, women, and children. Still the Bostonians' comparative leniency—many undoubtedly worshipped in lofty St. Botolph's Church—is certainly its own eloquent testimony.

The magistrates, said Bradford, treated the Pilgrims "courteously, and showed them what favor they could, but could not deliver [free] them till an order came from the [Privy] Council table" in London. This transmittal took some weeks. When it did arrive its moderation implies that the magistrates may have minimized the charges brought against the Pilgrims.

Bradford, in his summation, said,

"After a month's imprisonment, the greatest part were dismissed; and sent to the places from which they came: but seven of the principals were still kept in prison, and bound over to the assizes [court session]."

The cells where the seven Pilgrims were held—still to be seen—comprised the town jail, in the old Guild Hall. They have big barred doors and are windowless. A winding flight of stone steps leads up, through a trapdoor on the next floor, to the courtroom. The name of only one of the imprisoned seven leaders has come down specifically to us: William Brewster. This assize inquest led to no action and Brewster and the others were finally released.

How, after being stripped of their money, these Pilgrims were able to provide for themselves, we are not told. Their friends and former neighbors must have helped. By spring 1608 "some of these and others," who may have been those who furnished the necessary funds, were making new arrangements to escape to Holland.

The urgency was increased. Agents for the ecclesiastical authorities were also moving against them. One of their congregation, the grandson of Nottinghamshire's high sheriff, had been "clapped up in prison."

He had been charged, on November 10, 1607, as

Arrows show Pilgrims' route to Amsterdam as well as routes from Leyden to Delftshaven (years later) and on to England.

Pilgrims were confined in these cells in Guild Hall, Boston, England; steps at the right lead to the courtroom.

"a very dangerous, schismatical Separatist, Brownist, and irreligious subject, holding and maintaining divers erroneous opinions." For his "unreverent, contemptuous and scandalous speeches" to the court, he was immured in the castle at York.

Moreover, the bishops' pursuivants, messengers of the ecclesiastical court, had still other members of the Pilgrim congregation enmeshed. On December 1, 1607, one was charged with "disobedience in matters of religion," and on that same day William Brewster faced the same charge. Neither appeared in court but each was fined twenty pounds (half a year's pay in those days) and attachments were ordered.

Two weeks later, on December 15, the court's agent "certified that he could not find them, nor understand where they are." A peek into the Guild Hall's municipal cells in Boston might have given him the answer.

Once more the Pilgrims were preparing by springtime to leave Scrooby, leave their friends who had given them shelter, familiar scenes, the manor no longer in Brewster's possession, St. Wilfred's, the nearby ancient graveyard with its many memories. Not so long ago Brewster had buried his mother there in the little churchyard.

This time we know something of the way in which the Pilgrims went to meet a Dutch shipmaster who would take them aboard ship on the coast between Grimsby and Hull, then and now great fishing ports on either side of the Humber River with its estuary that enters the North Sea between the East Riding of Yorkshire and Lincolnshire.

The boarding place, unnamed, seemed secure, for it was in a remote location on the flat, marshy coast "where was a large common a good way distant from any town."

The Dutch shipmaster owned his vessel. The Pilgrims who made the arrangements had chanced upon him at Hull on the northern, Yorkshire side of the Humber. "They made agreement with him, and acquainted him with their condition, hoping to find more faithfulness in him than in the former [ship-master] in their own nation. He bade them not fear, for he would do well enough." And he did.

Scrooby is in the broad valley of the Trent River, which loops nearly 200 miles across the English Midlands. The Ryton River, a short distance north of Scrooby, is joined by another small waterway: the Idle River, which flows into the Trent.

The Pilgrim men placed women, children, and belongings in the boats on the Ryton and, on reaching the Trent, transferred them into "a small bark which they had hired." Then those men not needed to help manage the bark walked thirty miles across northern Lincolnshire to the isolated "large common."

The bark sailed twenty miles north on the Trent to where Yorkshire's Ouse River comes down from the north and together with the Trent forms the Humber River, flowing eastward to the sea. The "large common" was on the southside of the broad Humber estuary where it enters the North Sea, just north of Grimsby. The tides in the estuary are fast and forceful.

The passage was rough. The women became sea-sick "and prevailed on the seamen to put into a creek hard by where they lay on ground at low water"—a site now generally believed to have been Immingham Creek, five miles north of Grimsby.

They were a day early. Next day, when the Dutch shipmaster arrived off shore, "they were fast aground and could not stir until about noon." The shipmaster, meanwhile, seeing the men "walking about the shore," decided to save time and sent in a boat to fetch them on board. He was ready to send again for another boatload, said Bradford, who was among those already aboard the Dutch ship, when:

"The master espied a great company, both horse and foot, with bills [longhandled weapon and hooked blade] and guns and other weapons, for the country [local area] was raised against them. The Dutchman, seeing that, swore his country's oath, "Sacremente! and having the wind fair, weighed his anchor, hoisted sails, and away." Which was about all the shipmaster could sensibly do.

Misfortune had struck again. Spies, bounty seekers must have alerted the sheriff and constables and catchpolls. Now the misery was double—ashore and afloat.

The men most sought by the authorities—which would include Brewster and the Pilgrims' two Separatist clergymen—made shift to escape before the troop

Courtroom scene depicted on a wall in Guildhall shows the courtroom as it may have looked during the Pilgrim era.

Painting of a courtroom hangs in a former courtroom in Guild Hall, where Pilgrims faced trial.

could surprise them, those only staying that best might be assistant unto the women."

"Pitiful it was to see the heavy case of these poor women in their distress, what weeping and crying on every side, some for their husbands that were carried away in the ship . . . others not knowing what should become of them and their little ones; others again melted in tears, seeing their poor little ones hanging about them, crying for fear and quaking with cold."

On the ship, said Bradford, "the poor men were in great distress for their wives and children which they saw thus to be taken, and were left destitute of their helps; and themselves also, not having a cloth to shift [reclothe] them with, more than they had on their backs, and some scarce a penny about them, all they had being aboard the bark.

"It drew tears from their eyes, and anything they had they would have given to be ashore again, but all in vain, there was no remedy, they must thus sadly part."

Normally it is about 200 miles across the North

Sea to the narrow entrance past Texel Island into the old Zuider Zee (South Sea), thence some 50 miles south down this great gulf to Amsterdam, which at that time, despite the war with mighty Spain, was the thriving commercial heart of the most advanced and prosperous nation in Europe. But it was not how the trip to Holland went for these already profoundly distressed men.

En route, there arose "a fearful storm at sea" and they were uncontrollably driven near the coast of Norway 400 miles to the north. Their passage consumed two weeks and more before they reached land, and half of that time they "neither saw sun, moon, nor stars . . . the mariners themselves often despairing of life, and once with shrieks and cries gave over all, as if the ship had been foundered in the sea and they sinking without recovery.

"When the water ran into their mouths and ears and the mariners cried out, 'We sink, we sink!' they [the Pilgrims] cried, if not with miraculous, yet with a great height or degree of divine faith, 'Yet Lord Thou

Officials arrested many Pilgrims at Immingham Creek, disrupting their flight to Holland.

canst save! Yet Lord Thou canst save!' with such other expressions as I shall forbear.

"Upon which the ship did not only recover, but shortly after the violence of the storm began to abate, and the Lord filled their afflicted minds with such comforts as everyone cannot understand, and in the end brought them to their desired haven, where the people came flocking, admiring their deliverance; the storm having been so long and sore, in which much hurt had been done, as the master's friends related unto him in their congratulations."

Meantime, what happened to the women and children arrested at the creek?

"They were," said Bradford, "hurried from one place to another and from one justice of the peace to another, till in the end they [the authorities] knew not what to do with them; for to imprison so many women and innocent children for no other cause (many of them) but that they must go with their husbands, seemed to be unreasonable and all would cry out of them.

"And to send them home again was as difficult, for they alleged, as the truth was, they had no homes to go to, for they had either sold or otherwise disposed of their houses or livings [livelihoods].

"After they had been thus turmoiled a good while and conveyed from one constable to another, they were glad to be rid of them at the end upon any terms, for all were wearied and tired with them. Though in the meantime they (poor souls) endured misery enough; and thus in the end necessity forced a way for them. . . .

"And in the end, notwithstanding all these storms of opposition, they all gat over at length, some at one time and some at another, and some in one place and some in another, and met together again according to their desires, with no small rejoicing."

There was a special "fruit," Bradford said, from the "troubles which they endured and underwent in these their wanderings and travels both at land and sea." For in eminent places—Boston, Hull, Grimsby—"their cause became famous" because of their "godly carriage and Christian behavior" and they "greatly animated others" to follow their example. The Pilgrims could have had no greater delight, with their missionary zeal, than that their example should attract others.

Arriving in wartime Holland seemed to these newcomers, said Bradford, "like they had come into a new world—"fortified cities strongly walled and guarded with troops of armed men . . . a strange and uncouth language . . . different manners and customs of the people with their strange fashions and attires,

Amsterdam Harbor scene from the era of the Pilgrims' arrival from England

all so far differing from that of their [the Pilgrims'] plain country villages. . . ."

Their first views of Amsterdam, with the tower of its Oude Kerk (Old Church) dominating the scene from the harbor, must have been impressive indeed to these pastoral religious refugees. Formerly a small fishing village at the harbor's edge on the Amstel River, just off the Zuider Zee, Amsterdam had grown into a great metropolis during the Middle Ages—growth magnified by merchants and skilled artisans flowing from communities to the south, especially Antwerp, which had fallen under Spain's control.

Amsterdam's ready access to the sea made it a natural home port for Dutch explorers, for trading vessels and for shipping its manufactured goods. Navigators, among them the English explorer Henry Hudson, sailed from this harbor with Dutch seamen to seek both Northeast and Northwest passages to the Orient. Dutch ships were already bringing riches from the Far East, and final plans were about ready to establish a great world bank at Amsterdam—something then unknown in the British Isles.

Amsterdam, above all, was a haven from religious harassment. It also afforded potentially the nearest, most fruitful labor market available to these displaced, plundered, poverty-stricken English farmers.

The last to flee with the women and children across the North Sea were their leaders, Rev. Robinson, Rev. Clyfton, and Brewster, who had "stayed to help the weakest over before them." Now a new challenge arose for them in this cosmopolis-refuge that Bradford described as "flowing with abundance of all sorts of wealth and riches:

"It was not long," he recounted, "before they saw the grim and grisly face of poverty coming upon them like an armed man. . . ."

The newcomers, not being citizens, did not have access to membership in the guilds that controlled the best-paid employment. Nor did they have the required skills. For nearly all the only jobs available were the most modest-paying—jobs suited to beginners or the unskilled. But they were "armed with

The Pilgrims' escape to Holland in 1608 from Immingham Creek is memorialized on this marker.

faith and patience," were dependable, hardworking, uncomplaining.

Their presence in Amsterdam is associated chiefly with a narrow alley called the Street of the Brownists, between the Old Church (Oude Kerk) and the New Market—a section not far from the harbor where they had landed, in the oldest part of the city.

It was here they joined in communion with earlier immigrants in the Ancient Brethren who, before fleeing England, had organized the Ancient Church in London's Southwark. Rev. Francis Johnson, after his long imprisonment and escape from England, was again pastor of these Ancient Brethren.

Holland had welcomed thousands of religious refugees since the embattled William the Silent, a few years before Philip II's assassins murdered him, had declared to the magistrates of Middleburg: "You have no right to interfere with the conscience of anyone so long as he works no public scandal or injury to his neighbor."

The Pilgrims were eager to enjoy this religious freedom in peace, but within a year of their coming to Amsterdam they found that the harmony they had sought was threatened. Among the earlier English residents arose dissension over religious views.

Rev. John Smyth, who had fled from Gainsborough with his flock, fell into contention with his former college tutor, Rev. Francis Johnson. Rev. Smyth had come to believe that Scripture should be read in the original Hebrew and Greek and not in English. Further study led him to doubt that infant baptism was valid. He came to advocate self-baptism, and is known to history as Smyth the Se-Baptist.

These disputations were accompanied by flurries of contending religious tracts and sermons, publications that were freely permissible in Holland. The climax came for the Pilgrims when, Bradford observed, "the flames of contention were like to break out in that ancient church (Rev. Johnson's) itself, as afterwards lamentably came to pass."

Rev. John Robinson—increasingly admired for his peaceable nature, common sense, learning, and wise, amiable guidance—now became leader of the Scrooby flock when their original pastor, Rev. Clyfton, white-haired and much aged by his sufferings, decided to remain with Rev. Johnson and the Ancient Brethren. Bradford, who got his first religious teaching from Rev. Clyfton, said that "the reverent old man . . . was loath to remove any more."

The city of Leyden, twenty-five miles to the southwest and a haven where the Pilgrims would live for more than eleven years, was selected. Leyden, though then the second largest community in Holland, was less than half Amsterdam's size and did not have its easy access to the sea. Still the Pilgrims resolved to go "though they well knew it would be much to the prejudice of their outward estates . . . as indeed it proved to be."

Earning livelihoods would be much harder, a stern, unsuspected training for the harsh life that would one day confront them in the faraway New World wilderness.

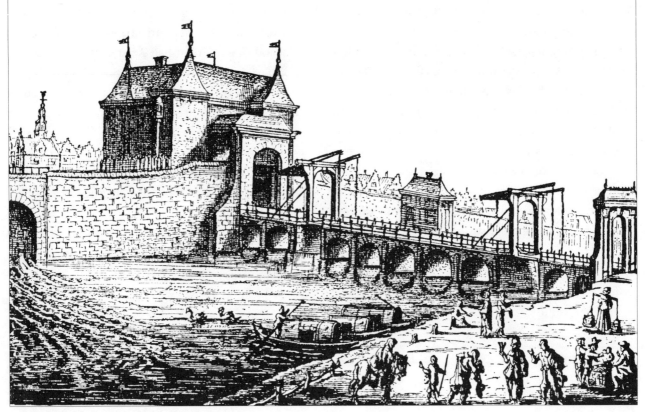

LEYDTSE POORT
La Porte de Leyden

Amsterdam gateway led to Leyden in the early 1600s.

King James
Hounds Pilgrims in Holland

Still in the Leyden Archives is the official action taken on the undated memorial, written in Dutch, which Rev. John Robinson sent to the Leyden magistrates, stating respectfully:

"Some members of the Christian Reformed religion, born in the kingdom of Great Britain, to the number of 100 persons or thereabouts, men and women, represent that they are desirous of coming to live in this city by the 1st of May next; and to have the freedom thereof in carrying on their trades, without being a burden in the least to any one."

Over the signature of one of their most respected leaders, Jan van Hout, the Leyden magistrates hospitably declared February 12, 1609, by way of response:

"They refuse no honest person free ingress to come and have their residence in this city, provided that such persons behave themselves, and submit to the laws and ordinances; and therefore the coming of the memorialists will be agreeable and welcome."

Not so to King James.

The Pilgrims had hardly bundled up their belongings and come the canal route to Leyden—passage westward toward Haarlem and then southwest to Leyden—when King James's ambassador at The Hague, only eight miles southwest of Leyden, informed the Leyden magistrates about King James's displeasure with their decision to admit these Brownists.

In the straightfaced, diplomatic manner, the magistrates sent the ambassador copies of the correspondence with Rev. Robinson, and claimed that they had acted "without having known, or as yet knowing, that the petitioners had been banished from England, or belonged to the sect of the Brownists . . . and request that we may be excused by . . . His Majesty."

This reaction was in the well-known liberal spirit of van Hout. The

Leyden magistrates, of course—long accustomed to furnishing haven to religious refugees and to supporting reformist activity in their already famous university—well understood the Pilgrims' plight. Also, a twelve-year truce the Dutch had signed in spring 1609 with Spain made subservience to the wishes of his Brittanic majesty less imperative.

King James, however, would play a far more punitive role against the Pilgrims during their stay in Leyden.

"Leyden . . . a fair and beautiful city and of a sweet situation, but made more famous by the university wherewith it is adorned, in which of late has been so many learned men." In those words Bradford pinpointed the community's chief attractions, particularly its professors' renown. One of them, Johannes Polyander, who would have an important part in the Pilgrims' difficulties with King James, in telling friends about his house on one of Leyden's numerous Venice-like canals lined with linden trees, added exultantly: "I am lodged in the most beautiful spot in the world."

Leyden, like much of the Dutch landscape, resembles low-lying meadow, save for an artificially raised hill where the two branches of the Old Rhine, flowing in from the east, join near the city's center and flow as one broader stream westward out of Leyden. On the hill, called the Burgh, was in early times a fort and later a castle.

When the Pilgrims came to Leyden its greatest fame was for the months-long siege its citizens had withstood in the war for independence from Spain. The Dutch tenacity, reduced to starvation, with rats and dogs their only food, and even those scarce, forced the Spaniards to withdraw when William the Silent cut the dikes and thus saved Amsterdam just to the north and made possible Holland's victory.

Quick employment was a critical need for the Pilgrim newcomers. Leyden had long been the center of the fine cloth trade. A lot of the wool goods exported from England, enriching ports like Boston, were manufactured into cloth in Leyden. In those days this industry did not mean that immense mills were built. Manufacture mostly meant work on hand looms in individual houses, with the clothing entrepreneur furnishing the working materials, then warehousing and trading the finished products.

Most of the Pilgrims got jobs in the cloth industry, the greatest number as weavers in wool, silk, linen, fustian, or bombazine. Some were wool combers and wool carders. Some made gloves, ribbons, and twine. A few were merchants. Some tried several jobs, ranging from baker to printer to tailor.

"They fell to such trades and employments as they best could," said Bradford, "and at length they came to raise a competent and comfortable living, but with hard and continual labor."

At first their lodgings were in the newer part of Leyden, a city that, like Amsterdam, was expanding as it prospered. Their costs were lowest there, in the northwest area of Leyden, and there the Pilgrims "pitched" (settled). Above all, they valued peace, said Bradford, and "their spiritual comfort above all other riches whatsoever."

"They continued many years in a comfortable condition, enjoying much sweet and delightful society and spiritual comfort together in the ways of God, under the able ministry and prudent government of Mr. John Robinson and Mr. William Brewster, who

This view of Leyden during the Pilgrim era shows the city's many windmills.

was an assistant unto him in place of an elder, unto which he was now called and chosen by the church.

"Such was the true piety, the humble zeal and fervent love of this people (whilst they thus lived together) towards God and His ways, and the single-hearted and sincere affection one towards another, that they came as near the primitive pattern of the first churches as any other church of these later times have done. . . ."

On May 5, 1611, Rev. Robinson and some members of the church, including his brother-in-law, completed purchase of a house "formerly called the Groene Port [Green Gate]" with a garden and a big vacant parcel of land in the rear. The purchase was made on behalf of the entire church, the price 8,000 guilders (equal then to 1,400 pounds), with one-fourth down and an annual mortgage payment of 500 guilders—a big debt.

Green Gate, which was used as a parsonage for

Rev. Robinson and his family, is the place most associated with the Pilgrim stay in Leyden, though it has long since been demolished. Here the Pilgrim congregation met and held its divine services. The house was in the old center of Leyden on the south side of the hoḟ (square) surrounding the foremost landmark in Leyden, St. Peter's Church, a former cathedral built early in the thirteenth century.

The house faced Bell Alley. The entrance to the old cathedral was just across the alley. A visitor leaving the house and turning left would very quickly arrive at the linden-bordered canal outside Professor Polyander's house, and by then crossing the bridge over the canal would arrive directly at the University of Leyden. Turn right on leaving Green Gate, and a walk of similar distance to the eastward would reach Leyden's main thoroughfare and another landmark, the Stadhuis (City Hall), an ornate medieval structure.

Green Gate, under lease when purchased, was not available to Rev. Robinson and the Pilgrims for another year. But the big vacant parcel of land was accessible and the carpenter member of the Church, William Jepson, began constructing twenty-one small dwellings on two sides of the land, a sort of "hof" of its own, for members of the church.

Rev. Robinson moved into Green Gate May 1, 1612. None of the Pilgrims left a description, but we can readily imagine their Thanksgiving service or their springtime gathering in the garden behind Green Gate with its well, which was the watering place for all those surrounding small dwellings built

An almshouse was built on the site of Green Gate, Leyden, where Reverend Robinson lived and the Pilgrims worshipped.

Garden area in the courtyard of the almshouse is the site where Pilgrim carpenters built twenty-one small dwellings.

by Jepson. Bradford has left a happy picture of Robinson and his flock:

"His love was great towards them; and his care was always lent for their best good, both for soul and body. For beside his singular abilities in divine things, wherein he excelled; he was also very able to give directions in civil affairs, and to foresee dangers and inconveniences: by which means he was very helpful to their estates; and so was, every way, as a common father to them."

Bradford and other Pilgrims obtained their marriage licenses at Old City Hall, Leyden.

The many extant records at the City Hall—public records of marriages, citizenship, real estate, mortgages—furnish vivid glimpses of Pilgrim life in Leyden.

Bradford became a citizen of Leyden in the year Rev. Robinson took over Green Gate. Now of age, Bradford had come into an inheritance from his family estate in Austerfield. He arranged to acquire a house of his own and in the following year walked with his witnesses up the magnificent City Hall staircase for his marriage to Dorothy May, sixteen-year-old daughter of the elder of the Ancient Brethren of Amsterdam. Bradford was twenty-three.

Bradford tells how "many came unto them [the Pilgrims] from divers parts of England, so as they grew to a great congregation." In all, they grew during their time in Leyden to some 300 parishioners. Word of the Pilgrims had gone far beyond the "eminent places" near Scrooby—Boston, Hull, and Grimsby. Newcomers came from Amsterdam's Ancient Brethren—and also from London and from shires Yorkshire to Kent.

The new members comprised some of the most prominent of the Pilgrims.

There was Isaac Allerton, a young London tailor, who would become a merchant and magistrate in the New World. Three would become deacons in Leyden: Robert Cushman, a wool comber from Canterbury; Samuel Fuller, silk-satin-and-serge maker from London; and John Carver, a Yorkshire merchant and brother-in-law of Rev. Robinson. Also there was Edward Winslow, London printer, a future governor in the New World.

The names of all these, save Carver, are on the marriage rolls—nearly four dozen Pilgrim weddings at Leyden. Carver, who would be the first governor of the Pilgrims in the New World, had married the older sister of Rev. Robinson's wife before coming to Holland.

Nearly 100 children were in the Pilgrim church during their time in Leyden—a delightful domestic picture. They were contemporaries of the future artist Rembrandt, a child in Leyden in those years. A far from joyful side was there, too. Childbirth was often fatal in those times. Burial records tell sad tales. Saddest is that of a friend of Brewster, Thomas Brewer, who within two months lost a child and then his wife and another son in childbirth.

The Pilgrims' simple, steadfast, industrious way of life brought them "good acceptation" from their neighbors:

"Though many of them were poor," said Bradford, "yet there were none so poor but that if they were known to be of that congregation [Brownists], the Dutch, either bakers or others, would trust them in any reasonable matter, when they wanted money; because they had found by experience, how careful they were to keep their word; and saw them so painful [painstaking] and diligent in their callings. Yea, they would strive to get their custom [business], and to employ them above others in their work, for their honesty and diligence."

In back of the land where the Pilgrims built the twenty-one small houses was the former Veiled Nuns' Cloister. The Leyden magistrates assigned its lower floor as the gathering place for the Reformed Scotch Church. The broadminded pastor of the Pilgrims, Rev. Robinson, was friendly with the minister and members of this Scottish church, and they would at times hold communion together.

Rev. Robinson's scholarship, like his tolerance, attracted many admirers, especially in the university. Soon after his arrival in Leyden Rev. Robinson, like many other exiled clergy on coming to Holland, published his opinions. He wrote a book, *A Justification of Separation*, a theological defense of noncompliance with England's state church. He frequented the university library, conveniently located on the upper floor in the nearby old Veiled Nuns' Cloister.

In the fall 1615 Rev. Robinson was admitted to the university as a "student of theology." Many advantages accompanied this honor—tax exemption, exemption from service in the city guard, an allowance of ten gallons of wine every three months and 126 gallons (half a tun) of beer every month—mighty welcome in an era without tea, coffee, soft drinks, or generally safe water supply.

Rev. Robinson delivered three university lectures and won "much honor and respect." Still the grateful university refrained from heaping any "public favor" on Rev. Robinson to avoid "giving offense to the state of England," namely King James.

Brewster, who had suffered the "greatest loss" in the Pilgrims' flight from Scrooby to Holland, had financial difficulties that were more burdensome because of his age. During those early years in Holland "he suffered much hardship," said Bradford, adding:

"He had spent the most of his means, having a great charge [expenses] and many children; and, in regard of his former breeding and course of life, not so fit for many employments as others were; especially such as were toilsome and laborious. But yet he ever bore his condition with much cheerfulness and contentation [contentment]."

Brewster's schooling at Cambridge came to his aid. He could speak in Latin, the scholars' tongue. The University of Leyden drew many students from Denmark and Germany. Brewster prepared a book of rules, in Latin-grammar style, and taught English in his dwelling. "Many gentlemen, both Danes and Germans," said Bradford, "resorted to him, as they had time from other studies: some of them being great men's sons."

Brewster's greatest help, however, came from Thomas Brewer, a wealthy gentleman from Kent who came to live in Leyden, in a house he purchased in Bell Alley just a door but one from Rev. Robinson's Green Gate. It was called Green House.

Brewer, a man in his late thirties, about ten years younger than Brewster, was a member of the Reformed Scotch Church. He was a Puritan zealous to spread the gospel. He made his house a center for students, among them a future minister in his church and a doctor. Brewer himself was enrolled in the University of Leyden as a scholar in literature.

Chiefly with Brewer's financing, Brewster was able late in 1616 to make arrangements for printing in his dwelling in Stink Alley, a narrow passageway off Choir Alley. The L-shaped, three-family structure had an entrance on Choir Alley, which runs from the main city street with its City Hall to the square surrounding St. Peter's Church, entering the square toward the rear of the church.

Brewster and his helpers had "employment enough," said Bradford; "and by reason of many books which would not be allowed to be printed in England, they might have had more than they could do."

Financial aid made it possible for Brewster, who was not a printer himself, to secure a master printer from London, John Reynolds. With Reynolds came an apprentice printer, or assistant, who would become a most eminent Pilgrim. He was Edward

Winslow, then twenty-one. They both lived in Brewster's house, and when they soon went with their brides to be married at the City Hall, members of the Brewster family went as their attendants.

Brewster's publications were far more religious than commercial. The first few books, in Latin and Dutch, bore his name, the date 1617, and the name Choir Alley in Latin: *In Vico Chorali*, the name most associated with these Pilgrim printing activities. That none of these first three books was in English and that only these bear the Brewster imprint indicates that they were intended to provide the operation with protection.

Eventually some dozen and a half books came from Choir Alley, which would keep such a small enterprise intensely busy. Later events, when the authorities raided the premises, suggest that no presswork was done in Choir Alley and that the type, when set, was taken for presswork to Dutch printing shops.

Late in 1618, with Europe about to be plunged into the devastation and agony of the Thirty Years War, and with Prince Maurice of Orange eager for English assistance, King

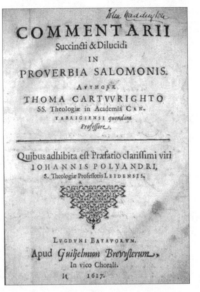

Brewster's first book, Commentaries, *a Latin commentary on religious proverbs, carries a preface by Professor Johannes Polyander.*

James was able to get the Dutch ruler to issue a *placaat* (edict) that prohibited foreigners in Holland from printing books objectionable to friendly foreign countries. King James was thus trying to extend his control over the press to Holland.

James had reason. Early in that year, in August, he had called a church synod held at Perth, the ancient capital of Scotland, in an effort to impose a hierarchy of bishops over the presbyters, the elders in the Scottish church. The Scots were unalterably opposed.

The historian of the Scottish church, nonconforming David Calderwood, wrote a tract denouncing the Perth Assembly as a nullity. To get it printed, he fled to Holland. In a few months, *Perth Assembly*, printed with type from Brewster's fonts, appeared in Scotland. The tract had been smuggled into Scotland concealed in wine vats. King James was incensed.

The Captain of the Guard in Edinburgh, on the king's orders, searched the "booths and houses" of three booksellers there but found neither *Perth Assembly* nor the author. An innocent Scottish bookseller who happened to be in London was seized and brought before the angry king.

"The devil take you away, body and soul," raged the king to the kneeling bookseller," for you are none of my religion." As for his Scottish subjects in general, the angry king added: "The devil rive [split] their souls and bodies all in collops [sliced meat], and cast them into hell!" The bookseller, who had no association at all with publishing *Perth Assembly*, was unjustly kept in prison for three months.

In July 1619, His Majesty's ambassador at The Hague, Sir Dudley Carleton, came across copies of *Perth Assembly* and some clues. He hurried off a message to Whitehall Palace to James's Secretary of State, Sir Robert Naunton, "I am informed it is printed by a certain English Brownist of Leyden, as are most of the Puritan books sent over, of late days, into England." In view of the new Dutch *placaat*, Carleton said he would complain to the Dutch authorities.

Five days later Carleton hustled off another note to Naunton in which he said that the culprit was "one William Brewster, a Brownist, who hath been, for some years, an inhabitant and printer at Leyden; but is now within these three weeks . . . gone back to dwell in London . . . where he might be found out and examined." If Brewster was not the printer, advised Carleton, "he assuredly knows both the printer and author."

Carleton was right. Brewster was already in England and three months earlier—doubtless aware of the royal manhunt—had, as Pilgrim deacon Robert Cushman, then in England, wrote the Pilgrims back in Leyden, gone "into the north" of England. Brewster, sought by the authorities in three countries, had discreetly gone underground.

Now began something of a comedy of errors. The

sleuths were unquestionably misled by friends of Brewster, particularly his friends at the University of Leyden, where his tutoring of scholars had made him quite popular.

Naunton wrote to Carleton that Brewster was not to be found in London, that he must be somewhere in Holland. Carleton wrote back to Whitehall that he was informed that Brewster was not only not in Leyden but unlikely to be, "having removed from thence both his family and goods. . . ."

From King James came something more menacing for the Dutch, eager for his good will. The king had commanded him, Naunton said, to tell Carleton to "deal roundly [vigorously] with the States General [the Dutch central government] in his name, for the apprehension of him, the said Brewster, as they tender His Majesty's friendship."

Carleton began to get hints that Brewster was in Leyden . . . no, maybe Amsterdam. He had searches made, keeping Naunton (and, of course, the irritated king) informed by successive messages. Then suddenly Carleton triumphantly informed them that Brewster had been taken in Leyden. But Carleton was quickly forced to get off another message, explaining that he was in error, an error caused by a bailiff, "a dull, drunken fellow [who] took one man for another."

The man under arrest was Brewster's benefactor, Thomas Brewer.

Brewer told the authorities that "his business heretofore had been printing, or having printing done" but blandly explained that he had quit any printing in the prior December because of the *placaat* making it illegal. He identified Brewster as "his partner," but, by way of throwing the pursuers off the

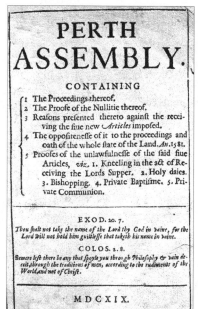

Perth Assembly *(title page shown)* denounced King James's effort to impose a hierarchy of bishops on the Scottish church.

Sir Dudley Carleton, King James's ambassador at The Hague, was a key figure in the search for Brewster in Holland.

scent, he said that Brewster was "in town at present, but sick."

The bailiff, now certainly sober, rechecked and reported that Brewster "had already left" Leyden. Brewer, "being a member of the university," was now transferred to the university authorities. When the bailiff asked assistance from the university to help him seize the illegal printing supplies the university officials—most likely with tongue in cheek—appointed Professor Polyander, Brewster's friend, to help the bailiff.

They found "the types" in the garret of Brewster's former dwelling in Stink Alley. They catalogued the books. They found the bailiff had "the garret door nailed in two places, and the seal of the said officer, impressed in green wax over the paper, is placed upon the lock and the nails. . . ."

Naunton wrote consolingly to Carleton:

"I am sorry that Brewster's person hath so escaped you; but I hope Brewer will help you find him out."

Brewer did no such thing.

The questioning of Brewer did not satisfy King James. He sent word from Hampton Court, by Naunton, that he would like to have Brewer remanded to England, and he would also like the States General to republish its *placaat* to prevent the "vending underhand [secret sale] of such scandalous and libellous" publications as *Perth Assembly*.

The king's request ran headlong into difficulties raised by the university. Its officials were unwilling to remand Brewer; they felt they should be the ones to try him. Carleton got the Prince of Orange to speak personally with the university rector. Finally Polyander arranged a compromise:

Brewer was to go "voluntarily" to England with the assurance that he could return to Holland within three months free of expenses, unharmed in person or purse.

Carleton called Brewer "a professed Brownist" who had "mortgaged and consumed a great part of his estate . . . through the reveries [dreams] of his religion." Questioning of Brewer in London proved futile. Naunton wrote Carleton that Brewer "did all that a silly creature could to increase his [King James's] unsatisfaction." Brewer was discharged.

But he did not go back to Holland.

A few years later Brewer, persecuted by the bishops for aiding gatherings of nonconformists in Kent, was fined 1,000 pounds and imprisoned. He was confined in King's Bench Prison for fourteen years until he was released by act of the Long Parliament, just before the Civil War against King James's son and successor, King Charles I.

Brewster, in heading "into the north," may well have avoided a much worse fate than Brewer's with King James—called the "wisest fool in Christendom" by the chief minister for a French monarch—thirsting for his arrest.

Stained-glass window depicts the destruction of the Pilgrim press in Brewster's house in Leyden.

Pilgrim Woes Mount

The prospect that the Pilgrims must once again uproot themselves, despite its subjecting them again to heartache and hazards, had become increasingly clear as far back as fall 1617.

It was not "any newfangledness or other such giddy humor" that impelled them. Their leaders, Rev. Robinson and Elder Brewster, and "the sagest members began both deeply to apprehend their present dangers and wisely to foresee the future and think of timely remedy." They were becoming profoundly distressed and felt that for "weighty and solid reasons" they must leave Holland.

The reasons did not slight in the least the benevolent reception they had received from the Dutch people. The Pilgrims prized their neighbors' high esteem. But they had come to realize that their economic future was insecure and that their English way of life—still loved by these religious exiles—was doomed if they remained in Holland.

"The grave mistress of experience . . . taught them many things," said Bradford of their years in that country. Bradford and another future New World governor, Edward Winslow, carefully marshaled the Pilgrims' experiences as the reasons that would eventually convince them that they should migrate to the New World.

Earning a living in handicrafts was hard—so hard that some who had come to join them had departed from Holland, and others who would like to join them "preferred and chose the prisons in England rather than this liberty in Holland." The Pilgrims were coming to feel convinced that "if a better and easier place of living could be had, it could draw many and take away these discouragements."

"The people generally bore all these difficulties very cheerfully . . . yet old age began to steal on many of them; and their great and continual labors, with other crosses and sorrows, hastened it before the time. It was not only probably thought, but apparently seen, that within a few years more they would be in danger to scatter, by necessities pressing them, or sink under their burdens, or both. . . .

"Many of their children . . . were oftentimes so oppressed with their heavy labors that though their minds were free and willing, yet their bodies bowed under the weight of the same, and became decrepit in their early youth, the vigor of nature being consumed in the very bud as it were.

"But that that was more lamentable, and of all sorrows more heavy to bear, was that many of their children, by . . . the great licentiousness of youth in that country, and the manifold temptations of the place, were drawn away by evil examples into extravagant and dangerous courses, getting the reins off their necks and departing from their parents.

"Some became soldiers, others took upon them far voyages by sea, and some worse courses tending to dissoluteness and the danger of their souls, to the great grief of their parents and dishonor of God. So that they saw their posterity would be in danger to degenerate and be corrupted.

"Lastly (and which was not least), a great hope and inward zeal they had of laying some good foundation, or at least to make some way thereunto, for the propagating and advancing the gospel of the kingdom of Christ in those remote parts of the world; yea, though they should be but even as stepping stones unto others for the performing of so great a work."

Winslow had additional reasons. Public education had long been a tradition in Holland, but the Pilgrims felt they could not give "such education to our children as we ourselves had received." The Dutch, as pictured in their happy genre paintings, treated Sunday as a day for pleasure and merrymaking. Brewster felt the stricter Pilgrims were not likely to succeed "in reforming the Sabbath." Another worry: "How likely we were to lose our language and our name, of English."

His last fear was prophetic. Only about a third of the Leyden congregation would eventually leave for the New World, and those remaining would, in little more than a generation, be completely assimilated into the Dutch melting pot.

The Pilgrims discussed every aspect of what they should do. They fasted and prayed for the Lord "to direct us." They were well aware of New World exploration and of "ill success and lamentable miseries befalling others"—Sir Walter Raleigh's lost colony, Roanoke; the failed Popham Colony in Maine. They also knew of Raleigh's latest—and futile—efforts in Guiana; Henry Hudson's discoveries in the future New York; and his friend Captain John Smith's then recent 1614 exploration in a region he christened "New England." And they knew at first hand about the current difficulties in early Jamestown, then the only English plantation in all North America.

They talked of New World dangers from savage people "cruel, barbarous and most treacherous . . . not being content only to kill and take away life, but delight to torment men in the most bloody manner. . . ." They talked about their paucity of funds "to fit them with necessaries." Yet with God's help they believed "the dangers were great, but not desperate; the difficulties were many but not invincible."

Still another trouble loomed. Holland's twelve-year truce made in 1609 with Spain was drawing to a close. Already, religious strife had begun in Bohemia that would lead to shocking desolation in the Thirty Years War. Already in their daily lives:

"There was nothing but beating of drums and preparing for war; the events whereof are always uncertain. The Spaniards might prove as cruel as the savages of America; and the famine and pestilence as sore here as there; and their liberty less to look out for remedy."

For a time division arose among them. Some favored going to the "perpetual Spring" in Raleigh's Guiana. Others feared its hot, unfamiliar climate and danger of Spanish attack. Some were for Southern Virginia and the Jamestown region. But then they feared they would again encounter the religious persecution that had driven them from England. The majority therefore determined to "try to live as a distinct body by themselves" in Northern Virginia (an area that then encompassed today's New England).

Optimistically, they resolved to attempt, with friends' help, to beseech King James "that he would be pleased to grant them freedom of religion."

Unknown to them, their negotiations would drag wearisomely over about three years.

First, they sought permission, a patent, from the Virginia Company of London, sponsors of the Jamestown Plantation. Through Elder Brewster they had some influential friends, especially Sir Edwin Sandys. Son of the late Archbishop of York, Sandys had been a friend of Brewster's father and was Brewster's landlord at Scrooby Manor.

Rev. Robinson and Elder Brewster, to aid in seeking a patent, drafted "Seven Articles" briefly stating the Pilgrims' views on the faith and form of the state church. Their adroit wording wisely showed submission to King James, and assented to the bishops' right to "govern them civilly." Their religious differences in that way were diplomatically minimized.

Two Pilgrim deacons, John Carver, fifty one, merchant, brother-in-law of Rev. Robinson; and Robert Cushman, thirty-nine, wool comber, were sent to London on the mission to get the patent.

Sandys was soon, on November 12, 1617, writing back to Robinson and Brewster that the two deacons had conducted themselves with "good discretion." The Seven Articles had given "good degree of satisfaction" to the gentlemen of the Council for the Virginia Company who had been approached by Carver and Cushman. The deacons had gone back to Leyden for more consultation, with the petition seemingly in "all forwardness."

Rev. Robinson and Brewster wrote back their thanks to Sandys and told him "that, under God, above all persons and things in the world, we rely upon you; expecting the care of your love, counsel of your wisdom, and the help and countenance of your authority." They sent him additional information about the Pilgrims that he might care to "impart to any other of our worshipful friends of the Council for Virginia."

The Pilgrims, they wrote, "believe and trust the Lord is with us. We are well weaned from the delicate milk of our mother country and inured to the difficulties of a strange and hard land. The people are . . . as industrious and frugal, we think we may safely say, as any company of people in the world."

"We are knit together, as a body, in a most strict bond and covenant of the Lord . . . we do hold our-

Sir Robert Naunton, King James's secretary of state

selves straitly tied to all care of each other's good, and of the whole, by everyone; and so mutually. It is not with us as with other men whom small things can discourage or small discontentments cause to wish themselves home again.

"If we should be driven to return [from the New World], we should not hope to recover our present helps and comforts: neither indeed look ever, for ourselves, to attain unto the like in any other place, during our lives; which we are now drawing toward their periods [ends]." They certainly appeared to be, as they would prove, reliable colonists.

Sandys procured help from the most highly placed friend, Sir Robert Naunton, King James's Secretary of State—the very official who would in less than two years be involved in James's unrelenting efforts to track down Brewster as the suspected printer of *Perth Assembly*.

Naunton urged the king "to give way to such a people, who could not so comfortably live under the government of another state, to enjoy their liberty of conscience under his gracious protection in America: where they would endeavor the advancement of His Majesty's dominions and the enlargement [spread] of the Gospel. . . ."

King James thought this "a good and honest motion" and asked Naunton how these people hoped to make profits in Northern Virginia.

"Fishing," replied Naunton.

"So God have my soul! 'tis an honest trade! it was the Apostles' own calling!" responded the king.

Prospects for the patent and their request for "Liberty in religion . . . confirmed under the king's broad seal" looked surprisingly favorable. The Pilgrims were told as much. Indeed, to help resolve some lingering questions in the Privy Council, Rev. Robinson and Brewster wrote an additional letter about Pilgrim church practices so that another highly placed friend, a wealthy London merchant, could use it to help their cause. The merchant even informed the young messenger who brought their letter that there was:

"Very good news, for both the King's Majesty and the bishops have consented."

But the merchant was mistaken and even Sir Edwin Sandys, for Sandys told the messenger to be at the next court [meeting] of the Virginia Company. But it turned out that the king afterward told Naunton that the Pilgrims "should confer with the bishops of Canterbury and London." Final advice of their friends, though, was to avoid doing that. Instead, the Pilgrims were urged to go ahead with their plans in the hope the king would leave them alone.

"In sounding His Majesty's mind," their friends told them they had found "that he could connive at [with] them, and not molest them; provided they carried themselves peaceably: but to allow, or tolerate, them by his public authority, under his seal, they found it would not be."

Carver and Cushman bore this report back to Leyden and it immediately "made a damp on the business." Again there was soul-searching and lengthy debate. Those intending to sell their property feared the king's implied promise might prove a "sandy foundation" on which to build their hopes. Others argued that even had they got the king's seal it could be revoked. The Pilgrims finally came to a decision bespeaking their faith:

"They must rest herein on God's providence as they had done in other things."

They would persevere. Some began to sell their property. Bradford sold his house by the back canal. This time Brewster and Cushman were sent to London with instructions "upon what conditions they should proceed with them [the Virginia Company]; or else to conclude nothing without further advice."

It was spring 1619 before Brewster and Cushman arrived in England.

1625 memorial in St. Mary's Church, Rotherhithe, depicts a Pilgrim-era vessel.

They were to find unexpected tribulation. The political cleavage that would later lead to civil war in England—and to heavy migration by Puritans to establish the Massachusetts Bay Colony—had now split the Virginia Company into two bitter factions, pro-king and prerogative against pro-people and Parliament.

In April Sir Thomas Smith, the ardent royalist who had headed the East India and the Moscovy trading companies as well as the Virginia Company of London, decided to cut down on his responsibilities, until he discovered that Sir Edwin Sandys was seeking to replace him as Virginia Company governor and treasurer. Smith strenuously opposed Sandys.

"Choose the devil, if you will, but not Sir Edwin Sandys," vehemently declared the king, but Sandys won the treasurer's position. The struggle, though, went right on, with James's Privy Council ordering house arrests, with threatened duels nipped at the eleventh hour, with a royal inquiry into the government of Virginia, and eventually with King James annulling the charter and taking over the Virginia colony.

Little wonder that Cushman wrote dolefully back to Leyden, on May 8, 1619, that he was withdrawing to his old home grounds in Canterbury to wait, for the "dissensions and factions were so extreme no business . . . could be despatched."

Cushman had two other pieces of news for Leyden:

—"Master B is not well at this time. Whether he will come back to you or go into the north, I yet know not." Cushman's Master B was, of course, Brewster, avoiding arrest. Copies of *Perth Assembly* were being uncovered in Scotland by the authorities. Brewster's going underground had been eminently prudent.

—Cushman's other information was "heavy news." Word had just reached London from the west of England that Francis Blackwell had died along with 130 out of 180 passengers "packed together like herrings" into a vessel headed for Jamestown. Blackwell, well known to the Pilgrims, was ruling elder of a dissident remnant of the Ancient Brethren Church in Amsterdam.

Blackwell was blamed for packing so many into the ship when it left Gravesend, at the mouth of the Thames River, toward the beginning of the prior winter. The ship was driven far off course by storms. The passengers lacked water and food and were plagued by dysentery. The survivors barely made port in March after the ship's captain and six marines died.

Before leaving England, Bradford wrote, Blackwell had been arrested "with sundry godly citizens" at a private religious gathering. When taken before the church authorities he "dissembled" about his faith and was able thus to "slip his own neck out of the collar" by informing against other nonconformists, including the Pilgrims' young messenger, who was promptly arrested.

Bradford's comment on Blackwell's behavior:

"He so won the bishop's favor, but lost the Lord's, as he was not only dismissed, but in open court, the Archbishop gave him great applause, and his solemn blessing to proceed in his voyage. But if such events follow the Bishop's blessings, happy are they that miss the same."

Cushman, in breaking the tragic news about the perils in voyaging to the New World, wrote in his letter, "I would be glad to hear how far it will discourage you. I see none here discouraged much, but rather desire to learn. . . . It doth often trouble me to think that, in this business, we are all to learn, and none to teach; but better so, than to depend upon teachers as Master Blackwell was."

The Leyden faithful, characteristically, were far from discouraged.

On May 26, 1619, their petition for a patent was referred to Sandys's committee at his house in London. On their friends' advice the patent was requested in the name of a stranger to the Pilgrims, Rev. John Wincop, chaplain to the Earl of Lincoln. The Puritan leaning of Sandys was self-evident. The Earl's household was also Puritan and would in the coming decade be intimately connected with the Puritan migration to Massachusetts Bay. In the household lived a future Bay governor, Thomas Dudley, the earl's steward; and a visitor was another future Bay governor, John Winthrop.

The Wincop patent received the official seals June 9, 1619. But the long, agonizing ordeal for the Pilgrims was still not over.

The Virginia Company for some time had been

eager to make tracts of land available to "planters" (settlers). Jamestown had thus far failed as an investment and bankruptcy for the company was just five years away. Securing the patent, of course, provided none of the financial help, supplies, and shipping that the Pilgrim pioneers so desperately required.

Meantime the threat of war grew. In August, King James's son-in-law, Frederick, Elector of the Rhineland-Palatinate and leader of the Calvinist Reformation forces, was offered and accepted the crown of Bohemia—an action that would set in motion against Frederick the Holy Roman Empire's mighty imperial armies.

Wealthy Dutch merchants now learned of their Pilgrim residents' considerable needs and they made tempting proposals to Rev. Robinson when he informed these merchants that he was ready to induce more than 400 families, both from Holland and England, to live in the New Netherland region on the Hudson River. The merchants even offered free shipping and free cattle for each family.

The imminent war prompted the Pilgrims to inquire if Holland would also give them two warships for protection. To get the ships, the directors of the New Netherland trading company on February 2, 1620, petitioned Prince Maurice of Orange, son and successor of the assassinated William the Silent. The Pilgrims emphasized the advantages to Holland. The Dutch had been trading for furs for several years on the Hudson River but had no plantation as yet, "only factors [agents] there, continually resident, trading with the savages." The Pilgrims could be the first settlers and hold New Netherland for Holland!

Prince Maurice, already drilling for war, was hardly in a position to spare two warships. But before he made his decision—and it would be to reject the directors' petition—there came, providentially, a most lively visitor to Leyden who quickly, with Aladdin-like magic, convinced the Pilgrims that he would satisfy their most pressing needs.

He persuaded them: "Not to meddle with the Dutch proposal" and not "too much to depend on the Virginia Company."

Then, if they were still resolved to migrate, "he and such merchants as were his friends, together with their [the Pilgrims'] own means, would set them

forth: and they should make ready and neither fear want of shipping nor money; for what they wanted should be provided."

The visitor, Thomas Weston, a London ironmonger, was a highly compelling character, chockful of the Elizabethan age's high spirit, a promoter, a speculator. Weston for some time had been a leader and treasurer for a group of similar London men, merchant adventurers, joint stockholders in moneymaking pursuits from fishing to trading shipments of wool to the Low Countries. The latter adventure, when it had run afoul of the licensing monopoly held by a different group of London merchants, had fetched Weston's group a rebuke from the Privy Council.

Without Weston's appearance at this time it is highly doubtful that the Pilgrims would have been on their way to the New World in 1620. Weston did have shortcomings. He was an overpromising, overoptimistic enthusiast. His profoundest motivation was strictly moneymaking, and writings and propagandizing by Captain John Smith had convinced Weston that money was to be made in the New World.

It so happened that Weston had a hand in a patent that an associate of his, John Peirce, a London cloth entrepreneur, had obtained February 2, 1620, from the Virginia Company of London. It is likely that this Peirce patent was more liberal than the Wincop patent—a moot matter, for both have disappeared.

Weston advised the Pilgrims to use the Peirce patent. He also asked them to draw up a contract of terms, not especially for him, but for his fellow adventurers. Articles of agreement were thereupon drafted and Weston promptly approved them.

The joint-stock arrangement with the adventurers, ten pounds value to the share, could be in cash paid in; or every colonist going who was more than sixteen years of age would represent a share, and any colonist defraying the cost of his own provisions would rate a share. Two children between ages ten and sixteen years of age would rate a share, and every child under ten would rate "50 acres of unmanured land." All profits and benefits from the plantation would go into a common property to be divided proportionately at the end of seven years.

Deacons Carver and Cushman were dispatched to England "to receive the monies and make provision both for shipping and other things for the voyage: with this charge [injunction], not to exceed their commission [instructions] but to proceed according to the . . . Articles of Agreement. A committee was chosen at Leyden to do the same thing. More Pilgrims planning to go now sold belongings, and those few who were able put money into shares of the common stock.

At about this time the Pilgrims in Leyden learned from Weston and others that the old Virginia Company of Plymouth in the west of England was being reorganized and was about to get a royal charter to the area in Northern Virginia now being called "New England."

Further word came that Weston leaned to having the Pilgrims locate their plantation in New England. This proposal revived division and debate. Some once again pressed the idea of going to Guiana, others to Southern Virginia. Some "merchants and friends that had offered to adventure their monies, withdrew; and pretended many excuses."

Far worse news was that the adventurers in England had demanded some changes in the contract. Weston, on his return to London, found some of his associates unwilling to venture their money unless the Pilgrims agreed that the common stock should include even their private dwellings and their improved lands, and they must agree to work seven, not five days a week for the common property.

Rev. Robinson, learning about this harsh development, said that including private houses, gardens, and house lots in the common property would represent but a "trifle" to the adventurers but would be "a great discouragement" to the emigrants, who would have to "borrowe hours from their sleep" to make the houses comfortable. The other demand, he felt, was shortsighted, too—"a new apprenticeship of seven years and not a day's freedom from task!"

Cushman, in London, confronted with the possibility that the bottom would fall out of the whole project if he rejected Weston's new demands, gave his approval. This decision would sharply divide the Pilgrims and the adventurers, impairing and even threatening to destroy their cooperation, and it brought Cushman's independent action under Pilgrim criticism that was not entirely just.

Cushman, sorely upset, wrote to Leyden that he knew of the "great discontents and dislikes of my proceedings" for "making conditions fitter for thieves and bond slaves than honest men." He said he was so busy "I cannot be absent one day, except I should hazard all the voyage." But, he assured them, when they should come together "I shall satisfy any reasonable man." And he pleaded:

"Only let us have quietness and no more of these clamors."

Suspicions now arose about Weston. The voyage committee in Leyden, which included Bradford and Winslow, wrote Cushman, "Salute Master Weston from us, in whom we hope we are not deceived." Even Rev. Robinson felt doubts. In a letter in mid-June 1620, Rev. Robinson said that Weston did not have "shipping ready before this time . . . cannot in my conscience be excused."

Weston, as his group's treasurer, was plainly having trouble raising money. He had undoubtedly grasped at the idea of a New England colony because a fishing monopoly might go with it, meaning quick profits. But when that possibility eluded him he probably embraced the harsher terms to retain and attract investors. Several times he told Cushman that "save for this promise he would not meddle at all with the business any more."

Weston, like Rev. Robinson, was worried about the passage of time. Quite properly, Weston objected that provisions for the voyage were being assembled in three places: by Cushman in London, by Carver at Southampton, and in Kent by a newcomer, headstrong Christopher Martin of Essex, who had been appointed to the task to represent the many "strangers" (non-Pilgrim group emigrants) recruited by the London adventurers to go on the voyage.

Cushman said that Weston complained:

"We will, with going up and down, and wrangling and expostulating pass over the summer before we will go." The eventual loss of good-sailing time would be dangerously far worse.

The Leyden committee had acquired a sixty-ton vessel and had it refitted, in particular with large new masts. It was called *Speedwell*. Rev. Robinson said that Weston had made "himself merry with our endeavors about buying a ship." Weston, of course, had far more experience with ships than the Leyden ex-farmers.

Acquiring the ill-fated *Speedwell*, though, did seem a sound idea. It could provide the Pilgrims a consort across the vast ocean and, once in the New World, could be used for fishing and trading ("trucking," they called it) and for "such other affairs as might be for their good and benefit of the colony when they came there."

"Pitiful" feelings were now replaced by hope when Cushman sent word to Leyden that a pilot had been sent over, Master Reynolds should stand by to bring the *Speedwell* and its passengers to Southampton, and another pilot had been hired, Master John Clarke, "who went last year to Virginia with a ship of kine [cattle] from Ireland." Then, still in June, moving at the last minute to save expenses, Weston and Cushman hired a 180-ton vessel owned and berthed at Rotherhit, a very active port on the south side of the Thames River two miles east of London Bridge. This ship was the *Mayflower*.

Mayflower Sets Sail— At Last

P rayer—an appeal for God's guidance—came first into the Pilgrims' minds upon receiving the news that their migration to the New World was finally to get under way.

"They had a solemn meeting and a day of humiliation, to seek the Lord for His directions," said Bradford. Their pastor, Rev. Robinson, preached a sermon recounting the Biblical story of how "David asked counsel of the Lord." Rev. Robinson then spoke comforting words, "strengthening them against their fears and perplexities; and encouraging in their resolutions."

Even if they were already to go together they lacked the "means to have transported them." They decided that if a majority had their affairs ready for departing, then Rev. Robinson would accompany them as their pastor. If not, they desired that Brewster, who was in communication with them, would go as their elder.

Those going would "be an absolute church of themselves, as well as those that stayed, seeing, in such a dangerous voyage and a removal to such a distance, it might come to pass they should, for the body of them, never meet again in this world. "Still, all would continue members in Holland or the New World without any further dismission or testimonial."

Winslow told of two other major decisions made by the congregation at this time: "They that went should freely offer themselves" and "the youngest and strongest part" should go first.

Another day of solemn humiliation was held when notice came from Delftshaven—a port near Rotterdam on the River Maas a little more than twenty miles south by canal—that the *Speedwell*, with its new masts and sails, was ready.

Rev. Robinson, the beloved pastor, preached his final sermon for the departing Pilgrims. He read a lesson from the Bible that to seek God was "a right way for us and for our children. He spent a good part of the day very profitable and suitable to their present condition," said Bradford, and there were fervent prayers "mixed with abundance of tears."

Winslow also recalled some of Rev. Robinson's words:

"Whether the Lord had appointed it or not, he charged us before God and his blessed angels, to follow him no further than he followed Christ."

The broadminded pastor exhorted them that "if God should reveal anything to us by any other instrument of His, to be as ready to receive it as ever we were to receive any truth of his [Robinson's] ministry; for he was very confident the Lord had more truth and light yet to break forth out of His holy word.

"Another thing he commended to us, was that we should use all means to avoid and shake off the name of Brownist, being a mere nickname and brand to make religion odious . . . and to that end, said he, I would be glad if some godly minister would go over with you before my coming."

Rev. Robinson, who would be frustrated and prevented from ever coming to the New World, told them, "Be not loath to take another pastor or teacher . . . for that flock that hath two shepherds is not endangered but secured by it." The Pilgrims would hope for years that Rev. Robinson would rejoin them, but in vain, and his role of teacher for the departing minority would be filled by the Elder Brewster.

Those who were to stay in Leyden feasted those who were to go. The feasting, with the sermon and praying, was in the pastor's large house "where," said Winslow, "we refreshed ourselves, after our tears, with singing of psalms, making joyful melody in our hearts as well as with the voice . . . indeed it was the sweetest melody that ever mine ears heard."

Next day most of this close-knit fellowship made the canal passage together, moving through Delft, Dutch capital and burial place for the martyred champion of their religious freedom, William the Silent. In

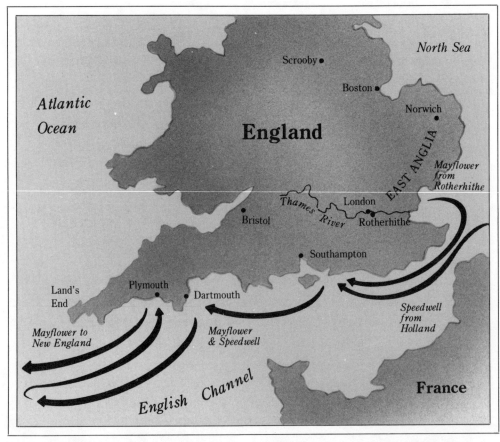

Arrows show the routes of the Speedwell *and the* Mayflower *to Southampton and then to Dartmouth and Plymouth, England; the* Mayflower *finally set out for the New World alone.*

a final remark on their departure from Leyden, Bradford gave them the name by which they would generations later become known to history.

"They knew they were Pilgrims," he said, "and they looked not much back on the pleasant city that had sheltered them, but lift up their eyes to the heavens, their dearest country, and quieted their spirits." Their final hours with their friends—for most would never again see one another on earth—were poignantly related by Bradford:

"When they came to the place [Delftshaven], they found the ship and all things ready; and such of the friends as could not come to the New World with them, followed after them; and sundry also came from Amsterdam to see them shipped, and to take their leave of them.

"That night was spent with little sleep by the most, but with friendly entertainment, and Christian discourse, and other real expressions of true Christian love.

"The next day, the wind being fair, they went aboard and their friends with them; when truly doleful was the sight of that sad and mournful parting. To see what sighs and sobs and prayers did sound amongst them; what tears did gush from every eye, and pithy speeches pierced each heart: that sundry of the Dutch strangers that stood on the quay as spectators, could not refrain from tears.

"But the tide, which stays for no man, calling them away that were thus loath to depart; their Reverend Pastor, falling down on his knees, and they all with him, with watery cheeks, commended them, with most fervent prayer, to the Lord and His blessing. And then, with mutual embraces and many tears, they took their leaves one of another; which proved to be the last leave to many of them."

A martial touch was recalled by Winslow, for all ships—in fear of pirates—traveled armed in those days.

"We gave them [the well-wishers]" said Winslow, "a volley of small shot [musket fire] and of three pieces of ordnance. And so lifting up our hands to each other; and our hearts for each other to the Lord our God, we departed—and found His presence with

The Embarkation at Delfthaven, *by Robert W. Weir, depicts Pilgrims holding service prior to departure.*

us, in the midst of our manifold straits that He carried us through."

It was Saturday, July 22, 1620, Old Style. The *Speedwell* went past the Hook of Holland and across the North Sea to the English Channel. They had a "prosperous wind" and in a short time the small ship entered the great harbor at Southampton, where the Pilgrims found that the *Mayflower* from London was already berthed with the "Strangers," who would comprise the rest of their company.

They found "a joyful welcome and mutual congratulations," said Bradford, "with other friendly entertainments. . . ."

There were familiar faces, Carver and Cushman, so long away on months of negotiation and preparation. And most of all there was their elder, Brewster—though he was constrained to adopt some disguise until distance should give him a feeling of security from sudden arrest by the pursuivants of the bishops or the king's officers.

This was the first meeting between Pilgrims and Strangers—men, women, and children recruited mostly in and around London, East Anglia, and the southeastern section of England.

For most of the Strangers, though they would become known as Pilgrim forefathers, the attractions offered them by the adventurers were chiefly economic—a chance to own land of their own, to escape poverty being spread in England by inflation and by farmers being forced from their farmland for the more profitable raising of sheep.

If all the hired hands and servants were excluded, the Strangers would come close to outnumbering the Pilgrims.

A notable Stranger, Captain Myles Standish—in his mid-thirties, short, robust, with florid countenance—had served with the English volunteers who fought in Holland to aid the Dutch. He would become the Pilgrims' celebrated military right arm in the New World. Two other Strangers would become assistant governors: Stephen Hopkins, who had already made one trip to the New World and been shipwrecked in Bermuda; and Richard Warren, a London merchant.

The Strangers brought problems, too: profane John Billington of London, whom the Pilgrims would

The Mayflower Inn on the site of Rotherhithe Wharf is where the "Strangers" boarded the Mayflower.

have to hang a decade later for murder; and Hopkins's two young servants, who would fight a duel.

The five hired hands were a cooper and four sailors. The cooper, a twenty-one-year-old blond man from East Anglia, was John Alden. Alden would settle in the New World and marry the daughter of a Stranger, Priscilla Mullins, who would utter the legendary words to her hesitant lover, "Why don't you speak for yourself, John?"

The Pilgrims' lean purse and the adventurers' tightfisted behavior accented money problems at Southampton. They were compounded by differences that arose among the three men obtaining the provisions—at three places, which had evoked shrewd disapproval from enterprising Thomas Weston.

Especially disturbing to Cushman, who had the impossible assignment of diplomat, too, was Christopher Martin's attitude. Martin, named a purchasing agent to represent the Strangers, had been chosen treasurer by the adventurers. A stubborn man, Martin purchased freely, without consulting the Pilgrim agents, and drove Pilgrim financing into a muddle that years of effort would fail to clarify or correct.

Cushman said that nearly 700 pounds had been spent at Southampton "upon what I know not." Master Martin, Cushman protested, "saith, he neither can, nor will, give an account of it. And if he is called upon for accounts, he crieth out of unthankfulness for his pains and care, that we are suspicious of him: and flings away. . . . Who will go and lay out money so rashly and lavishly as he did, and never know how he comes by it?"

Ominously, the *Speedwell*, which had shown some sailing quirks on the passage from Holland, cut into the Pilgrims' skimpy funds. It had to be "twice trimmed at Southampton."

The worst moments at Southampton, though, came with Thomas Weston's arrival and his efforts to get the emigrants to agree to the altered seven-year contract demanded by some of the adventurers. On this issue, the irascible Martin felt like the people from Leyden. The adventurers, Martin told Cushman, "were bloodsuckers!" Martin must have meant this label for all the others, for he had ventured 50 pounds himself.

Captain John Smith, in his *General Historie*, wrote that the adventurers were about seventy in number— "some gentlemen, some merchants, some handicraftsmen, some adventuring great sums, some small, as their estates and affections served." They were a voluntary combination, not a corporation, and "dwelt mostly about London."

The adventurers well knew, Smith said, that establishing a plantation could not be done "without charge, loss and crosses." Thomas Brewer, who had financed Brewster's publishing, was among the adventurers. A few Pilgrims were adventurers. Some of the adventurers later were among these who formed the Massachusetts Company that led to settlement of Boston. Many at this juncture would "adventure no more" because the general stock had already cost 7,000 pounds.

Weston, clearly not an entirely free agent, was "much offended" when the Pilgrims told him that he knew right well the original terms and that they had been enjoined when they left Leyden not to agree to any new terms "without the consent of the rest that were behind."

Then when they told Weston that the enterprise needed "well near 100 pounds" to clear Southampton, he told them he would not dispense another penny. He promptly headed back to London, telling the Pilgrims angrily that they could now "stand on their own legs."

After a discussion, the conscientious Pilgrims wrote a letter to the merchants and adventurers, making a new compensating offer.

They expressed their sorrow that "any difference at all be conceived between us." They said that the possibility of owning their own houses and lands "was one special motive, amongst many others, to provoke us to go" and also that they never gave Cushman assent to make the change. Still they offered:

"That if large profits should not arise within the seven years, that we will continue together longer with you, if the Lord give a blessing."

They understood, they said, that three-fourths of the adventurers were not insisting on the harsher terms; as for their own plight:

"We are in such strait at present as we are forced to sell away 60 pounds worth of our provisions, to clear the haven [the port]; and withal put ourselves upon great extremities; scarce having any butter, no oil, not a sole to mend a shoe, nor every man with a sword to his side; wanting [lacking] many muskets, much armor, etc. And yet we are willing to expose ourselves to such eminent dangers as are likely to ensue, and trust to the good Providence of God. . . ."

Captain Smith, a tireless promoter of plantations in New England, put in perspective what the Pilgrims were about to do. Since his 1614 explorations in New England, its fame had grown so "that 30, 40, or 50 sail went yearly, only to trade and fish.

"But nothing would be done for a plantation till about some 100 of your Brownists of England, Amsterdam and Leyden, went to New Plymouth: whose humorous ignorances caused them, for more than a year, to endure a wonderful deal of misery with an infinite patience; saying my book and maps were much better cheap to teach them than myself."

Smith had offered his services to the Pilgrims and been turned down. After all, they did not think they were headed for New England, and Weston and Cushman had already hired pilots who had been to the New World. And anyway, they did indeed have Smith's book and maps.

Departure this time included no farewells from friends.

A governor, with two or three assistants, was chosen for each of the vessels "to order the people . . . and to see to the disposing of the provisions and such like affairs." All this arrangement was agreeable to the skippers of the ships. Master Martin was chosen governor for the *Mayflower*, Deacon Cushman for the *Speedwell*.

About the only ceremony was calling together all the company to hear a letter that had arrived from Rev. Robinson. He wished he could be with them. He had final words of advice, especially because they were about to govern their own affairs, that they chose people who "do entirely love and will promote the common good . . . yielding unto them all due honor and obedience in their lawful administrations. . . ."

The two vessels sailed August 5—belatedly, but not disastrously late if all now went well.

But they had not gone far before Master Reynolds found the *Speedwell* so leaky "he durst not put further to sea till she was mended." He signaled Master Christopher Jones of the *Mayflower*, came

aboard the larger vessel to confer, and they decided to put into the port of Dartmouth for repairs.

Master Reynolds had abundant grounds for worry. Cushman, feeling ill, being deeply disturbed trying to justify his accepting the oppressive seven-year contract, and upset by Martin's high-handed treatment of the Pilgrims and sailors aboard the *Mayflower*, wrote of his troubles to a friend in London. In the letter he told about the *Speedwell*'s shocking condition.

"She is as open and leaky as a sieve, and there was a board, two feet long, a man might have pulled off with his fingers, where the water came in as at a mole hole. . . . If we stayed at sea but three or four hours more she would have sunk right down."

The necessity for twice trimming the *Speedwell* at Southampton had consumed an extra week of fair weather. "Now we lie here waiting for her in as fair a wind as can blow. . . . Our victuals will be half eaten up, I think, before we go from the coast of England, and if our voyage last long, we shall not have a month's victuals when we come in the country."

Bradford said that the *Speedwell* was "thoroughly searched from stem to stern, some leaks were found and mended, and now it was conceived by the workmen and all, that she was sufficient, and they might proceed without either fear or danger." They set out again August 23 "with good hopes."

But all was not well. By the time they were more

Westgate in Southampton leads to West Quay, from which the Pilgrims sailed.

Plaque on Westgate tells of the Pilgrims' embarkation from West Quay on the Mayflower.

than 100 leagues [about 300 miles] at sea—into the Atlantic and far beyond land's end—Master Reynolds again signaled for a conference. Frantic pumping could "barely keep up with the leaks" in the *Speedwell*. Reynolds said that he must "bear up or sink at sea." And they turned back and put into the nearest big port, Plymouth Harbor, where they were certain to obtain expert help.

This harbor, in the western part of England and the English Channel, had long been famous in England's wars, seafaring, and worldwide exploration. The governor of both the fort and the port was a man of ancient English lineage, Sir Ferdinando Gorges, one of the foremost champions of establishing plantations in the New World.

Gorges, now in his mid-fifties, was a soldier knighted by the Earl of Essex on the battlefield—and a courtier having considerable influence with King James. At the very moment when the Pilgrims arrived in the port, Gorges had pending before the Privy Council his request for a new charter to convert the old Virginia Company of Plymouth into the Council for New England.

No one would be happier than Gorges to see two vessels entering his harbor, intending a voyage to the New World to begin a plantation. This endeavor was something Gorges had been trying to achieve since the beginning of the century, when a returning explorer, George Weymouth, presented Gorges some Indians—an event that aroused Gorges's hopes to use the Indians as interpreters and guides in founding colonies.

Gorges, who would become known as the "Father of Maine" though he never set foot in America, had steadfastly persisted in his efforts despite repeated and costly failures. Right now he was being forwarded reports from an explorer-trader-agent, Captain Thomas Dermer, whom he had sent to the Plymouth area shown on Captain John Smith's map, the identical area where these Pilgrims would by chance establish New England's first permanent English plantation.

The Pilgrims were well received by Gorges's people and the townspeople while the *Speedwell* was examined once again. Captain Jones, who was making his first trip to the New World, could only find conversation on exploration—and any reports from Captain Dermer—thoroughly helpful. Captain John Smith, whose map of New England was currently one of the best-known maps among English seafarers, had often sailed as Gorges's agent.

The finding on the *Speedwell* was, though, emphatically not good.

"No special leak could be found," said Bradford," but it was judged to be the general weakness of the ship, and that she would not prove sufficient for the voyage. Upon which it was resolved to dismiss her and part of the company, and proceed with the other ship. The which (though it was grievous and caused great discouragement) was put in execution."

Provisions and supplies had to be transferred from the *Speedwell*'s hold to the *Mayflower*. Worst wrench was that the number of passengers had to be reduced by twenty. Still, Bradford observed, "those that went

A model of the Mayflower *tops this memorial tower in Southampton.*

back were for the most part such as were willing so to do, either out of some discontent or fear they conceived of the ill success of the voyage. . . ."

Among them was Deacon Cushman, still ill and feeling the unmerited harassment he was bearing "like a bundle of lead . . . crushing my heart." Cushman had written to his London friend that he saw: "The dangers of this voyage . . . no less than deadly. Friend, he declared, "if ever we make a plantation, God works a miracle!"

Such, said Bradford, were Cushman's fears at Dartmouth; and he added, "They must needs be stronger now. . . ."

This was severe on Cushman. Bradford was equally severe on Master Reynolds. Bradford agreed that overmasting—putting excessively large masts into the reconditioned *Speedwell*—had naturally opened her seams when she was under heavy sail. But he suspected Reynolds had done this deliberately so that he and the crew, signed on for a year, could get out of their contract when supplies seemed to be falling low. In after years, Bradford writes, once the *Speedwell* was refitted she "made many voyages . . . to the great profit of her owner."

Again came a "sad parting," for neighbors from Leyden were going back to London on the *Speedwell*, and while in Plymouth the Pilgrims had been "kindly entertained and courteously used by divers friends."

Overall, the *Speedwell* venture had turned out ruinously in loss of time, and this loss, protracting the Pilgrims' passage into the raging autumnal Atlantic storms, would contribute to a dreadful toll of lives among the brave men and women and children—and tragically as well among the crew, now taking a farewell view from the decks of the crowded *Mayflower*.

Already it was some forty-five days since they had left Holland—sufficient time to have completed a normal Atlantic crossing—and the Pilgrims only now saw the sails raised and the vessel about to depart from old Plymouth Harbor.

It was September 6.

They had, said Bradford, "a prosperous wind which continued divers days together" as their passage resumed. Many, though, were soon "afflicted with seasickness." Soon they again passed Land's End and the Isles of Scilly. They were beyond the English Channel. Ahead of them—the only thing between them and the New World—was the Atlantic Ocean, a vast, awesome expanse.

To most of these essentially plain farm folks their real transport was more their faith in God than their vessel.

And of this faraway land they hoped to reach—their future home, they hoped—what was known to these Pilgrims in the year 1620? What had been discovered?

Earlier Explorers in Pilgrimland

B radford told of exploration in the future New England, in particular mentioning explorers from Bartholomew Gosnold, who christened Cape Cod, where the Pilgrims would make their first New World landfall, to ill-fated Thomas Dermer—Sir Ferdinando Gorges's man—who visited the Pilgrims' future Plymouth "but four months" before the Pilgrims arrived there.

Both England and France, whose long struggle for control over North America would eventually involve the independent existence of the Pilgrims' colony, were very slow in establishing permanent colonies. Spain moved comparatively fast after the discoveries by Christopher Columbus. England's New World claims were based on the 1497 voyage by John Cabot and his son, but more than a century would pass before Jamestown was founded in 1607.

Jamestown's very name—after King James I—emphasizes the great gap in time between the reign of Henry VII, who gave the Cabots a patent for their tiny ship's goal, and King James's religiously repressive reign. Indeed, even Queen Elizabeth, whose reign was made glorious by world-ranging discoverers, the "Virgin Queen" for whom Virginia was named, was dead some years before Jamestown was founded.

It was near the end of March 1602 that thirty-year-old Gosnold, intent on founding a colony, sailed from England with backing by, among others, William Shakespeare's patron the Earl of Southampton. Gosnold, like Sir Walter Raleigh and others before him, would fail—in fact, failure extended all the way back to the Norsemen if their Vinland included our New England.

Not until the Pilgrims started raising their shelters on land would New England have a permanent settlement and, at last, take root.

Future clergyman John Brereton, in the first English book published on

New England, gave his eyewitness account of Gosnold's voyage. Gosnold went where the Pilgrims would go. He entered the future Barnstable harbor, climbed the hills, discovered that the cape was part of the mainland, that "sundry islands" were to the south, and anchored at the tip of the cape.

There, said Brereton, Gosnold took such a "great store of codfish" that he named the headland "Cape Cod," and as for the islands, he named Martha's Vineyard after his then five-year-old daughter and the Elizabeth Islands for his sister Elizabeth.

Gosnold, though, was more interested in founding a colony. On the southernmost of his Elizabeth Islands, the one called Cuttyhunk by the Indians, he built a fortified house and traded with the Indians. But when he found no gold or copper mines he instead loaded his ship with cedar, skins, and sassafras, then a popular cure-all, and in June sailed back to England on finding that victuals were short and too few of his men were willing to stay.

So vanished the last chance for an English colony in North America in the Virgin Queen's reign.

In the immediately succeeding years explorers would come to the harbor and area where the Pilgrims would finally build their habitation. Twenty-year-old skipper Martin Pring, backed by Bristol merchants cheered by the profits from Gosnold's cargo of sassafras, began his voyaging to America in 1603, made a landfall in Maine, came down the coast and into the future Plymouth harbor.

Pring, unlike the Pilgrims, found no dearth of Indians in this place the Patuxet Indians called Accomack. The Indians came, said Pring, "sometimes 10, 20, 40 or threescore, and at one time 120 at once" and "they did eat peas and beans with our men." Pring built a barricade for his men, and was so im-

Cabot's embarkation from Bristol on the voyage that gave England its claims to North America

pressed by the strength and lightness of a seventeen-foot Indian birchbark canoe that he brought one back to Bristol. Pring lauded the area, the abundance of its trees, fruit, wildlife, fish, and "the goodness of the climate and of the soil."

The great French explorer Samuel de Champlain visited the future Plymouth harbor in July 1605, part of his voyages of discovery along the North American coast, harbors, and rivers that began in 1603 and would lead to the establishment of Quebec on July 3, 1608.

Again unlike the unpeopled Plymouth that the Pilgrims would find, Champlain saw a "great number of Indians" who came out in canoes to greet him. He named the place Port St. Louis for the patron saint of France and, as he did for other places he visited, he made a map of the harbor. On it he depicted the Indians' dwellings and gardens, indicating their large population before the plague struck them.

By the time the next major explorer, Captain John Smith, came to the same harbor, England had its first struggling and suffering colony in North America, Jamestown, but any colonization in Northern Virginia—the future New England—seemed to have suffered a mortal blow with the failed Popham colony of Sagadahoc by the mouth of the Kennebec River in Maine.

These two colonies, Jamestown and Sagadahoc, began in rivalry between two sponsoring companies in England, one in London and the other in western England in Plymouth. Jamestown got under way three months before settlers sent by the western England group, sponsored principally by Sir John Popham, Chief Justice of England, and Sir Ferdinando

Martin Pring built a barricade for his men at Patuxet, the future New Plymouth.

Monument at Cuttyhunk commemorates Bartholomew Gosnold, who named Cape Cod and the islands.

Gorges, landed in August 1607, and started building.

A fort went up at Sagadahoc—a storehouse, "meetinghouse, and some fifty shelters for the 120 expectant settlers headed by Sir John's nephew. Indians were friendly but the winter was severe, icy, bitter. Sir John, back in England, died. The nephew died, and when spring came all the remaining settlers embarked on a supply ship and on a new vessel they called the *Virginia of Sagadahoc*, first ship to be built in all Virginia, and went back to England.

Consequence in England:

"For any plantations," said Captain Smith, "there was no more speeches."

The enthusiast Captain Smith, though, never gave up. It was in 1614—six years before the Pilgrims—that Smith came to the future Plymouth. For years, as the burned fragment of a letter he wrote to Sir Ferdinando Gorges attests (a fragment now in the British Museum), Smith had been yearning to come to Northern Virginia. His colonial credentials were the best. He had been among the first settlers of Jamestown, became its willful governor, saving the colony before he left in 1609, and became its historian.

This time, in 1614, Smith was on an expedition with two ships financed by four London merchants "to take whales and make trials of a mine of gold and copper." They chased, but could catch no whales. There were no mines, and so they turned to fish and furs. While thirty-seven of his crew fished off Monhegan Island, Smith and eight or nine sailors ranged the coast, trading for beaver, martin, and otter skins.

"New England," said its namegiver, "is great enough to make many kingdoms and countries, were it all inhabited." On this famous exploration of the coast from the Penobscot River in Maine to the tip of Cape Cod, Smith found the Indians were friendly in general, and even after a scrap at the future Plymouth all again "became friends." In his search he found, he said, "Not one Christian in all the land."

Smith narrated his experiences along the coast in his *Description of New England*, published in London in 1616. He declared in summary—and repeated it in a later edition at the time the Pilgrims sailed—that "more than half [of the coast] is yet unknown to any purpose, not so much as the borders of the sea." As for the "goodness and true substance of the land, we are for the most part yet altogether ignorant of them," and only "God doth know how many thousand miles" they stretch inland.

In Smith's book was the famed map he made to illustrate his explorations. New England cartography now had a good foundation. Of earlier maps, Smith said that he had seen six or seven maps "so unlike each other, and most so differing from the true proportion or resemblance of the country, as they did me no more good than so much waste paper, though they cost me more."

To assist others journeying to New England, Smith gave assurance that he had drawn his map "from point to point, isle to isle, and harbor to harbor, with the soundings, sands, rocks, and landmarks as I passed close aboard the shore in a little boat."

Smith's laudatory dedication to Prince (later King) Charles reveals how English place names, some long part of the New England scene, got on the map. Smith reminded the Prince that it was Smith who had given Charles's and his brother Prince Henry's names to the Virginia headlands at the entrance to Chesapeake Bay. Smith asked Prince Charles, then fifteen years of age, to go over his New England map and change "barbarous names for such English, as posterity may say, Prince Charles was their godfather."

In sprinkling the names, Prince Charles, by chance, put Plymouth where Smith had indicated the Patuxet Indians' Accomack—and thus the future Pilgrim center already bore the name Plymouth when the *Mayflower* finally arrived there.

Captain Smith had told us of "a vile act" that occurred after he started back to England. The captain of the other ship in the expedition, Thomas Hunt, tried slaving on his own. Hunt treacherously took seven Nauset Indians and twenty Patuxets, the latter at the future Plymouth, and sold them as slaves in Spain. Monks at Malaga purchased the Indians their freedom. When the news of Hunt's villainy reached England, he was blacklisted in England "ever after from any more employment."

Hunt's slaving brought retaliatory misery to later seafarers coming to the New England coast. For the Pilgrims six years later it would bring difficulty and anxiety. Ironically, though, Hunt's despicable behavior preserved the life of an Indian vital to the Pilgrims,

Squanto, later described by Bradford as "a special instrument sent by God" to help the Pilgrims. Squanto, also known as Tisquantum, was among the Patuxets kidnapped by Hunt—and thus Squanto was saved from the plague that would destroy all others in his tribe.

Sir Ferdinando Gorges was, like Captain Smith, a man of phenomenal tenacity—even though, as a close friend of Sir John Popham, he had shared in the heavy losses at Sagadahoc.

The financial success met by Smith's 1614 voyage stirred Gorges and his intimates to try more expedi-tions. They sent Smith on two more of them, one defeated by a fierce storm and the other by French pirates' capturing him. During the week before Smith contrived his escape from the pirate ship, Smith used the time writing his account of his 1614 discoveries along the New England coast.

Smith's adversities still left Gorges undismayed. He even sent men to try Maine again, and they spent the winter at the present Biddeford Pool. That was the winter of the Indian plague, 1616 to 1617. The ship's captain called the place "Winter Harbor" and described the plague, which did not attack him or his

Statue of Captain John Smith stands in churchyard of St. Mary-Le-Bow Church in Cheapside, London, where he was a parishioner.

men, as being so catastrophic that it wiped out entire Indian villages.

In that summer, 1617, Gorges outfitted Captain Smith again, this time with "three good ships" to found a colony but, as Smith reported, his "design was frustrate" when a freak wind held him harborbound for three months "as was many a hundred sail [ships] more." Smith would make no more voyages of discovery.

One of these three ships, sent instead to Newfoundland for fishing, was commanded by a man of some consequence to the Pilgrims, Captain Thomas Dermer, who would be exploring for Gorges in the area of Plymouth just a few months before the Pilgrims' arrival at their future home.

Dermer, called an "understanding and industrious gentleman" by Smith, had been to the New World on several voyages.

When Dermer arrived in Newfoundland he encountered Squanto, who was trying to get back to his Indian kin at Accomack (Plymouth). Dermer at once saw this as an opportunity to help colonization and discussed it with the governor at Newfoundland, Captain John Mason, who later became known as the "Father of New Hampshire." Mason advised Dermer to consult Gorges. And so Dermer, with the consenting Squanto, headed back across the Atlantic to Plymouth, England.

As William Bradford would later, Gorges saw Squanto as help from Heaven. "It pleased God so to work for our encouragement again," said Gorges, "as He sent into our hands Tisquantum . . . formerly betrayed by this unworthy Hunt." Thus, said Gorges, "there was hope conceived to work a peace between us and his [Squanto's] friends, they being the principal inhabitants of that coast. . . ."

Gorges accordingly dispatched Dermer in 1619, along with Squanto, to join other Gorges ships in New England. Dermer, on arrival off Mohegan Island, found the ships gone. While most of his men and boys fished, Dermer with five or six men set off May 19 in a five-ton pinnace to explore the coast with Squanto as a guide.

"I passed alongst the coast where I found some ancient plantations, not long since populous, now utterly void; in other places a remnant remains, but

not free of sickness. Their disease: the plague, for we might perceive the sores of some that had escaped, who described the spots of such as usually die," Dermer wrote to England.

Smith, telling about Dermer's experience and the reports he had received—presumably from some of Dermer's crew—saw the mysterious plague's effects as an "advantage" to prospective planters. "God," said Smith, "had laid this country open to us, and slain most part of the inhabitants by cruel wars and a mortal disease; for where I had seen 100 or 200 people there is scarce 10 to be found."

Squanto was to find no kin to give him a homecoming. When he and Dermer arrived at the seat of the Patuxet tribe, where the Pilgrims would finally find asylum, they found "all dead." Of the Patuxets Squanto was the only survivor. Their cleared, untended lands at the head of Plymouth Harbor, Smith suggested, awaited newcomers.

Of this place Dermer wrote to Gorges: "I would that the first plantation might be here seated."

Dermer and Squanto went inland a day's journey to Namasket (present Middleboro) and found Indian inhabitants. Next day, Massasoit, the great chief of the Wampanoag Indians, with his brother and "a guard of 50 armed men" arrived. Squanto's presence made peace possible for the first time since the nefarious Captain Hunt aroused the Indians' understandable hatred. Dermer, on this visit, was even able to liberate from the Indians two Frenchmen shipwrecked three years earlier.

After sending home samples of the country's commodities and earth diggings (for his secret mission was still to find gold), Dermer sailed back to Monhegan and concluded business with the ships ready to depart, for he was planning to explore as far as Virginia. Dermer put Squanto ashore because Squanto "desired (in regard of our long journey) to stay with some of our savage friends at Sawahquatooke [present Saco, Maine]."

Squanto would be woefully missed.

At Monomoy on the Cape, Dermer was attacked by the Nauset Indians and, for a time, was held prisoner. Unlike the Wampanoags, the Nauset Indians had lost no warriors to the plague. Neither had Indians north of Maine's Penobscot River. Only

Indians between the Penobscot and Narragansett Bay—including, of course, the Massachusetts tribe at the future Boston—fell victim to this still unknown affliction. The Nausets remained bitterly disposed toward Europeans and capable of battle—as the Pilgrims would discover.

Dermer, with gold in mind, anchored at Capawack (Martha's Vineyard), and to his astonishment met a big, strong Indian named Epenow, who had reportedly been killed by gunfire five years earlier when Gorges sent him back seeking gold that Epenow assured Gorges was at Capawack. Dermer wrote that Epenow "gave me very good satisfaction in everything" and, with a fair wind springing up, Dermer took off for Virginia without pursuing Epenow's implied gold.

Dermer came back to the area just a few weeks before the Pilgrims left Delftshaven. Gorges, who received intermittent reports from Dermer and others, with the fishing and trading ships functioning as couriers, recounted what happened when Dermer met again with Epenow.

"This savage was so cunning, that after he had questioned him [Dermer] about me and all he knew belonged unto me, conceived he was come on purpose to betray him, and conspired with some of his fellows to take the captain. Thereupon, they laid hands upon him; but he being a brave, stout gentle-man, drew his sword and freed himself, but not without 14 wounds. This disaster forced him to make all possible haste to Virginia, to be cured of his wounds. At second return he had the misfortune to fall sick and die. . . ."

Commenting later when he learned what happened just prior to the Pilgrims' arrival, Bradford said it showed "what a peace it was that Dermer had made and "with what danger this [Pilgrim] plantation was begun, save as the powerful hand of the Lord did protect them."

Gorges said Dermer's death "much troubled me." Though that ardent royalist had none of the Pilgrims' religious motivation, still he shared their staunch determination to create a plantation in the New World. In less than two months after the *Mayflower's* departure from his harbor, Sir Ferdinando and his associates would receive a new charter from King James, and with it a grant that would include all of New England.

This charter incredibly included the entire territory between the 40th and 48th north parallels and extended westward sea to sea from the Atlantic Ocean—telltale of how little Europeans then really knew about this immense New World continent toward which the tiny *Mayflower* and the Pilgrims were headed.

The Pilgrims on the *Mayflower, by Henry Oliver Walker*

Mayflower
Anchors at Cape Cod

canny old seadog like Captain Christopher Jones could quickly catch the reassuring signs that the *Mayflower* was approaching land.

Crude instruments in his era left annoyingly uncertain the distance that a ship traveled each day. But at journey's end—when the leadsman's line, plunging fathoms below, touched seabed—the coastline could not be many miles away. Then the ocean color turned from sea blue to green, and old hands even claimed they could at last smell the still unseen land.

It was daybreak November 9, the sixty-fifth day since the *Mayflower* departed from Plymouth, England, and more than three anxious months since the Pilgrims had bade farewell at Delftshaven.

Suddenly came a shout from the lookout:

"Land ho!"

For those rushing on deck, the lookout stretched his arm toward the bluff above the shoreline that he had glimpsed over the ship's starboard bow.

The Pilgrim leaders described the scene most simply in *Mourt's Relation*, their first published account:

"By break of day we spied land. . . ."

Tears of relief, joy, and wonder came to many eyes as they looked toward the northwest—or gratefully to Heaven.

"The appearance of it much comforted us, especially seeing so goodly a land, and wooded to the brink of the sea. It caused us to rejoice together, and praise God that had given us once again to see land."

Captain Jones held a conference with the Pilgrim leaders. He had been roughly following the forty-second parallel toward land and felt certain that he was off Cape Cod. Explorers and skippers had been this way and he knew some of their tales.

RELÁTION OR

Iournall of the beginning and proceedings of the English Plantation setled at *Plimoth* in NEW ENGLAND, by certaine English Aduenturers both Merchants and others.

With their difficult paſſage, their ſafe ariuall, their ioyfull building of, and comfortable planting themſelues in the now well defended Towne of NEW PLIMOTH.

AS ALSO A RELATION OF FOVRE

ſeuerall diſcoueries ſince made by ſome of the ſame Engliſh Planters there reſident.

I. In a iourney to PVCKANOKICK the habitation of the Indians greateſt King Maſſaſoyt : as alſo their meſſage, the anſwer and entertainment they had of him.

II. In a voyage made by ten of them to the Kingdome of Nawſet, to ſeeke a boy that had loſt himſelfe in the woods : with ſuch accidents as befell them in that voyage.

III. In their iourney to the Kingdome of Namaſchet, in defence of their greateſt King Maſſaſoyt, againſt the Narrohigonſets, and to reuenge the ſuppoſed death of their Interpreter Tiſquantum.

IIII. Their voyage to the Maſſachuſets, and their entertainment there.

With an anſwer to all ſuch obiections as are any way made againſt the lawfulneſſe of Engliſh plantations in thoſe parts.

LONDON,

Printed for *Iohn Bellamie*, and are to be ſold at his ſhop at the two

Named for the unknown G. Mourt cited in its preface, Mourt's Relation *was the first book published about Plymouth Colony.*

The highlands of the future Truro, ten miles to the northwestward, were visible—an unmistakable Cape Cod landmark. The *Mayflower* was moving a safe distance off the beach along the "back side" of the Cape.

This landfall, most significantly, was quite a bit north of the area in which the Pilgrims were entitled to settle under the patent in their possession. After consultation, Captain Jones tacked about and headed the *Mayflower* south toward the intended destination in Northern Virginia—or, as Bradford related, "to find some place about Hudson's River for their habitation." Both wind and weather were fair.

As the excited passengers saw the land and were assured it was without doubt Cape Cod, Bradford observed: "They were not a little joyful." They surely had reasons in abundance.

Bradford, in all the wonderful history he would write years later from his eyewitness notes, did not mention the name of the vessel of which Captain

Jones was master. Still, in relating the emotion-filled departure of the Pilgrims from Leyden, Bradford did say that another vessel had been hired at London "of burden about 9 score." The records of Plymouth colony leave no doubt that this was the *Mayflower* of London of 180 tons.

No plan and no picture of the *Mayflower* remain. Still, London Port books and Admiralty Court records of the period provide facts about the ship and the master. Jones, who was part owner, had been her skipper for at least a dozen years, hauling cargo between England and both the Baltic Sea and the Bay of Biscay. Often this cargo was wine. A typical three-masted, squarerigged merchantman in the *Mayflower's* time and tonnage would be roughly ninety feet overall with beam of twenty-six feet.

Besides 102 passengers who crowded together on the *Mayflower* after the leaky *Speedwell* turned back, Captain Jones had a crew of twenty to thirty men. Their quarters would have been on the main deck, the top deck—the officers on the quarterdeck aft and the crewmen forward in the forecastle.

Unless Captain Jones, who was a considerate man, and his officers had extra tiers of bunks put in part of the steerage and poop house—quarters that these officers would normally use—all the 102 passengers would have had to squeeze themselves into the deck below, the gun deck, just over the vessel's hold.

We do know they had crowding. The Pilgrims' shallop (small sailing craft) had been broken down so that it could be carried on the gun deck. We know the shallop was used as emergency bunk space, possibly by as many as two dozen passengers, an unusual usage that would shortly cost precious time to get it back into repair.

Even a brief visit to Plimouth Plantation's replica of the *Mayflower*, *Mayflower II*, most often docked in Plymouth harbor close to Plymouth Rock, vividly demonstrates how crowded the sixty-five-day passage across the Atlantic must have been—with 102 passengers and their two dogs, a large mastiff and a small spaniel—jammed on the gun deck with its very low overhead.

Privacy, if it was possible at all, was minimal. Three of the women were pregnant, and certainly as they departed from England had reason to feel they

Pilgrims boarded the Speedwell *July 22, 1620, at this slip in front of* Oude Kerk *(Old Church), Delftshaven.*

Model shows Barbican area, Plymouth, England, at the time the Pilgrims sailed from here September 6, 1620.

Pilgrim Monument on Provincetown Highland commemorates the Pilgrims' first landing.

The Mayflower *and the* Speedwell *sailed August 23, 1620, from Bayard's Cove, Dartmouth, England, on their second attempt to cross the Atlantic.*

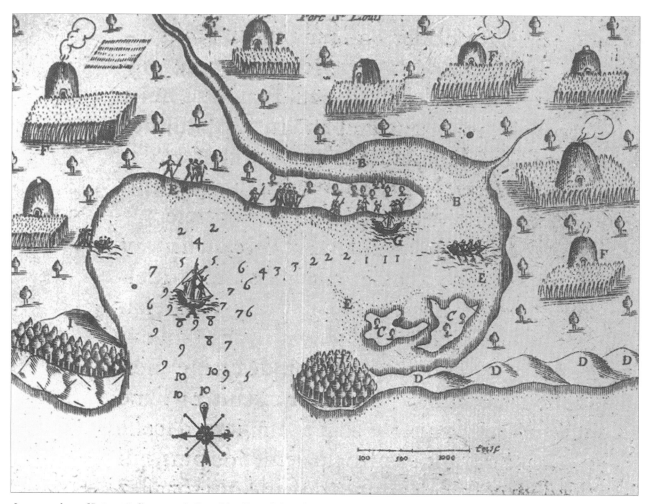

Large numbers of Patuxet Indians were indicated by Champlain in his 1605 map of future Plymouth Harbor.

John Alden and Priscilla, *by N. C. Wyeth, depicts the legendary Pilgrim lovers, who were married in 1622 and had nine children.*

A father shows his son how to shuck corn in Cornfield, *by N. C. Wyeth.*

The Pilgrims held their first meeting for public worship in North America on January 21, 1621 (lithograph by August Allebe after a painting by Johan Gorgeschwarze).

First Encounter, *by A. L. Whittaker, depicts the skirmish between the Pilgrims and Indians at Eastham.*

John Coggan, the first in a long line of Bay merchants, opened his store in Boston in 1634.

Rope making, vital to shipping, began in the colony in 1641 when John Harrison set up his "rope field" on Boston's Summer Street.

The Charter of the Province of Massachusetts, issued by William and Mary, united the Plymouth and Bay colonies.

Obelisk marker on Governor Bradford's grave atop Burial Hill overlooks Plymouth Harbor.

might encounter childbirth at sea. Thirty-two of the passengers were children, some of them babes in arms. Of eighteen couples, some like the Bradfords, had left children in Holland or England. Eight married men had left behind their wives. Also the passengers included adult single men, mostly hired hands and servants, and eleven unmarried women.

Comforts aboard were few, and they had no plumbing. The *Mayflower*'s nettings or buckets, to be emptied overboard, had to serve. Water for washing—save seawater—was severely limited. Changes of clothing were rare, even when wet, for the age of waterproof attire had not arrived. Heat was scanty, even in the crew's galley. Food was chiefly hardtack, salted pork and beef, cheese, and dried beans and peas. Tea, coffee, and chocolate were future comforts, and so for drinks they had chiefly water, even if a bit slimy, and beer.

When storms and howling winds were raging across the Atlantic, as they often did and the hatches and hatchways were covered and the gunports closed, the atmosphere on the lantern-lighted, heaving gun deck of even a ship called "sweet"—a legacy of its wine-carrying career—might have been mighty odoriferous as well as terrifying.

We have no log from the *Mayflower* and Bradford, who said he was seeking to "be brief," told of only a few happenings on the voyage. Soon after leaving Plymouth, he wrote, "many were afflicted with seasickness." But more interesting to Bradford was a "special work of God's providence" in solving another affliction the Pilgrims early encountered on shipboard: scorn and abuse from some of the crew toward these humble passengers who were given to praying and psalm singing.

"A proud and very profane young man, one of the seamen, of a lusty, able body . . . would always be contemning the poor people in their sickness and cursing them daily with grievous execrations." He never let up telling them that "he hoped to help cast half of them overboard before they came to their journey's end . . . and if he were by any gently reproved, he would curse and swear most bitterly.

"But it pleased God before they came half seas over," said Bradford, "to smite this young man with a grievous disease, of which he died in a desperate man-

ner, and so was himself the first that was thrown overboard. Thus his curses light on his own head, and it was an astonishment to all his fellows for they noted it to be the just hand of God upon him."

The most shocking moments came in mid-Atlantic. The Pilgrims had enjoyed "fair winds and weather for a season," but then many times there came "cross winds and . . . many fierce storms with which the ship was shroudly [severely] shaken, and the upper works made very leaky; and one of the main beams in the midships was bowed and cracked, which put them in some fear that the ship would not be able to perform the voyage."

Captain Jones, his officers, and the Pilgrims gathered in "serious consultation." Should they turn back? The sailors were divided; some were "loath to hazard their lives too desperately." Captain Jones, though, knew his ship best, that it had weathered many a crisis. He was positive that the *Mayflower*, despite leaky overhead, was "strong and firm underwater." The Pilgrims on leaving Holland had brought "a great iron screw" intended for help in raising pioneer dwellings. The broken beam was braced. The leaky deck was caulked.

They were confronted, however, with more loss of precious time. Captain Jones well knew danger if he tried to hoist too much sail. And so, said Bradford, "they committed themselves to the will of God and resolved to proceed."

They encountered several more storms, some with winds "so fierce and the seas so high as they could not bear a knot of sail, but were forced to hull [drift] for divers days together." Indeed, the *Mayflower*'s overall speed for their passage was less than two nautical miles an hour.

During one of these enforced drifts under short sail, twenty-eight-year-old John Howland, indentured servant of Deacon Carver and a future leader and magistrate of the Pilgrims, made his way from the crammed gun deck to the main deck. Suddenly, a pitch by the vessel flipped him overboard. Luckily he grabbed the halyard trailing from a topsail and, "though he was sundry fathoms under water" hung on until he was brought back aboard with a boat hook.

On the voyage across the Atlantic, late in the season when stormy waves swelled to ferocious heights dwarfing the *Mayflower's* masts, one birth and one death occurred among the passengers. A son, aptly named Oceanus, became the fourth child in the largest family on board, that of Elizabeth and Stephen Hopkins, recruited in London.

The passenger who died was a twenty-two-year-old indentured servant of Deacon Fuller, William Butten, who hailed from Bradford's village, Austerfield. Butten died November 6, less than a week before the Pilgrims caught sight of Cape Cod.

The *Mayflower* in the passage south along the Back Side of the Cape toward the Hudson River, had proceeded "about half a day" when suddenly, despite the weather being fair, "they fell amongst dangerous shoals and roaring breakers." Once again, as when the beam cracked in mid-ocean, the *Mayflower* was in deadly peril. The ship had come to the Pollock Rip shoals off Monomoy Point, southernmost part of Cape Cod and one of the Atlantic coast's most dangerous sections, then wholly uncharted and unmarked.

Even the great skill worked by a seasoned skipper such as Captain Jones could have been inadequate to save the courageous Pilgrims from shipwreck had not the wind turned "contrary" as night came on. The captain was able to bring the *Mayflower* about, then take her off the shoals, back into deep water and heading back north.

The Pilgrims, Bradford recounted, had "resolved to bear up again for the Cape and thought themselves happy to get out of those dangers before night overtook them, as by God's good providence, they did."

Cape Cod Harbor, now Provincetown Harbor, to which Captain Jones maneuvered hoping for safe anchorage, was up the fifty-mile length of the Cape's Back Side. But arrival there would confront the Pilgrims with a profound legal problem. Cape Cod Harbor, Bradford wrote, was not the permitted destination covered by their patent—for the *Mayflower's* heading would now bring them into Captain John Smith's "New England."

As the *Mayflower* sailed steadily northward on November 10, some of the Strangers began making "discontented and mutinous speeches . . . that when they came ashore they would use their own liberty for none had power to command them." The Pilgrim leaders moved promptly to quell this danger by drawing upon their own church experience in self-government and drafting covenants.

We do not know who wrote the Mayflower Compact. Only Elder Brewster, among all the Pilgrim leaders, was a university man. The Pilgrim writers best known to us are William Bradford and Edward Winslow, whose writings, first combined from their journals in *Mourt's Relation*, are the chief source for Pilgrim history.

Much of the sail on November 10 must have been devoted to discussing and preparing the Compact. The Pilgrims, after sacrifices they had already made, wanted to be certain beyond all doubt that law and order—"unity and concord," —would prevail once they reached shore. And to ensure this peace, the Compact was signed on shipboard before anyone disembarked, on the morning of November 11, when the *Mayflower* came around Long Point and Captain Jones ordered the anchor dropped "less than a furlong"—an eighth of a mile—from the point.

The Compact declared that they were forming "a civil body politic" to which all signers promised "due submission and obedience" to carrying out the purpose behind their voyage to plant the first colony in the northern parts of Virginia"—an objective they had undertaken "for the glory of God and advancement of the Christian Faith and Honor of our King and Country."

Until such time as they could get another patent, which John Pierce would obtain on June 1, 1621, from Sir Ferdinando Gorges and the Council for New England—the organization being formed as the *Mayflower* was leaving England—the Compact would be their only source of authority. Indeed, said Bradford, it was "the first foundation of their government" in the New World. Under it they pledged to enact and frame:

"Such just and equal laws, ordinances, acts, constitutions and offices, from time to time, as shall be thought most meet and convenient for the general good of the colony."

Forty-one of the passengers signed the Compact that morning. These included all thirty-four adult men among both Pilgrims and Strangers, three of the five hired hands, and four adult indentured servants.

That done, they thereupon confirmed John Carver, who replaced Christopher Martin as governor of the *Mayflower* for the voyage, to be their governor until next New Year's Day, then (under Old Style) the ensuing March 25. Carver, fifty-five-year-old former London businessman, had been a deacon of the Leyden church since 1617.

How eagerly and anxiously Pilgrim eyes must have scanned the harbor and the shore as Captain Jones brought the *Mayflower* to anchor.

In one of the most emotion-filled passages in his writings Bradford told how he could not but "stand half amazed at this poor people's present condition. . . ."

"Being thus past the vast ocean, and a sea of troubles before in their preparations . . . they had now no friends to welcome them nor inns to entertain or refresh their weatherbeaten bodies; no houses or much less towns to repair to, to seek for succor. . . .

"And for the season it was winter, and they that know the winters of that country know them to be sharp and violent, and subject to cruel and fierce storms, dangerous to travel to known places, much more to search an unknown coast.

"Besides, what could they see but a hideous and desolate wilderness, full of beasts and wild men—and what multitudes there might be of them they knew not.

"For summer being done, all things stand upon them with a weatherbeaten face, and the whole country, full of woods and thickets, represented a wild and savage hue. If they looked behind them, there was a mighty ocean which they had passed and was now as a main bar and gulf to separate them from all the civil parts of the world. . . .

"What could now sustain them but the spirit of God and His grace?

Signing of the Mayflower Compact, *by Edward Percy Moran*

First Landing, *by A. L. Whittaker, shows Pilgrims wading ashore in icy waters off present-day Provincetown.*

Troubles from the Cape
to Plymouth Bay

A t last in a "good harbor and brought safe to land," said Bradford, the Pilgrims "fell upon their knees and blessed the God of Heaven who had brought them over the vast and furious ocean, and delivered them from all the perils and miseries thereof, again to set their feet on the firm and stable earth, their proper element."

The longboat was put over the *Mayflower*'s side, and a landing party of fifteen or sixteen armed men headed for shore. But the longboat, with no landing place save in shallow water, could not get close to the beach, and the men, weighted with their armor and with axes to replenish the ship's exhausted wood supply, were forced "to wade a bowshot or two on going aland"—at least knee-deep in cold November seawater.

They were pleased with the large harbor and the wooded shore. "There was the greatest store of fowl that ever we saw" and whales "playing hard by us." The men climbed the highland where now the Pilgrim monument towers and saw the other, ocean side of the Cape, which reminded them of the dunes in Holland. Before returning that night to the *Mayflower* they "laded their boat with juniper," a chore that must have involved a lot of wading, for the sweet-smelling supply lasted the entire time that the *Mayflower* was moored in this harbor.

They were deeply eager to meet any inhabitants—potential future neighbors—but saw neither Indians nor any sign of Indian habitation.

The Pilgrims next day, a Sunday, remained steadfast in their religious devotion despite the pressure of time upon them. Ever since they had dropped anchor, Captain Jones and the crew had been urging that "with speed they should look out a place." Captain Jones did not want to leave until his passengers were without danger, but he had to keep a share of the diminishing food supply for his return trip. Others in the crew muttered

The first washday in the New World (a Monday) occurred at present-day Provincetown (painting by A. L. Whittaker).

that if the Pilgrims "got not a place in time, they would turn them and their goods ashore and leave them." These, though, lacked authority.

But Sunday was the Lord's Day to the Pilgrims and they observed it scrupulously in their customary devoutness.

On the following day, the Pilgrims went ashore "to refresh themselves and our women to wash, as they had great need." Thus did Monday as wash day become a long New England tradition. While the women scrubbed, the men fetched ashore the sections of the shallop, which was "bruised and battered . . . much opened with the people's lying in her."

The carpenters went to work to reassemble the craft on the beach. As with the *Mayflower*, we have no plan for the shallop. From its use in exploration and the number of passengers who would sail in it, the shallop—with single mast, mainsail, and jib—was probably between 20 and 30 feet long with a beam of 7 to 9 feet.

When it seemed that repair would take five or six days—and, actually, it would take much longer—some of the Pilgrims, "impatient of delay," desired to explore the shore, though without the shallop they would have to carry provisions on their backs.

Under solicitous instruction "to be out but two days," sixteen volunteers—with every man his musket, sword, and corselet (breastplate)—were put ashore on November 15 and set off in single file under their military leader: short, stout-hearted Myles Standish.

This was to be the first of three exploratory expeditions undertaken by the Pilgrims before—more than a month later—after many hardships, deadly exposure to the elements, Indian attack, tragic deaths, and near wreck of the shallop in a storm—the *Mayflower* would sail west across Cape Cod Bay and anchor in the harbor they finally chose for their plantation.

Standish and his men had gone a mile along the beach when they spotted five or six men and a dog. At first they thought these might be Captain Jones and some of his crew, who were also ashore. Then they realized that they were seeing Indians, they sought eagerly to meet with them. But the Indians, far fleeter then the armorclad Pilgrims, ran away.

After more miles of following footprints on sand and trails in woods, to no avail, the men prepared a lodging for the night, gathering wood, making a fire, and posting three sentinels. Next day, still within the future town of Truro, they resumed their trailing. They had brought only biscuits, Holland cheese, and a little bottle of aquavitae (liquor), and soon, having no water or beer, they were "sore athirst."

Presently, at mid-morning, they spotted a deer and came upon freshwater springs. Here they "drunk our first New England water with as much delight as ever we drunk drink in all our lives." Thinking then of the folks on the *Mayflower*, they headed for the beach and made a fire to signal back that all was well.

On first coming into Cape Cod Harbor, Captain Jones had spotted to the southeast what appeared to be a river opening into the mainland. The Pilgrims struck out southward to find it. En route they came upon none of the inhabitants they were hoping to meet but found evidence aplenty that this was Indian terrain. Near the present Pond Village they saw acres where the Indians had formerly planted corn, found Indian graves, then some planks where a house had been, and a large metal kettle.

Most providentially, they later spotted recently heaped mounds of sand and, after digging, uncovered a cache vital to their future: baskets of Indian corn and a few dozen ears of different colors. It was to them, said Bradford, "a very goodly sight, having never seen any such before." After agreeing that they would recompense the owners—which indeed they would one day do—they filled their pockets with the precious seed corn and also took the kettle, which two men carried away on a staff. The rest of the corn they reburied.

On nearing the river, now called after the local Pamet tribe, they saw the remainder of an old palisade, a fort—the handiwork of Europeans, as seemed true also of the planked house and metal kettle. As for the Pamet River, they felt that they had insufficient time to explore it and decided to leave that until they restored the shallop. They made note of two canoes, one on either bank, and then headed back.

That night, a very rainy one, they spent by the pond, after raising a barricade, making a great fire, and posting three sentinels. To save time in the

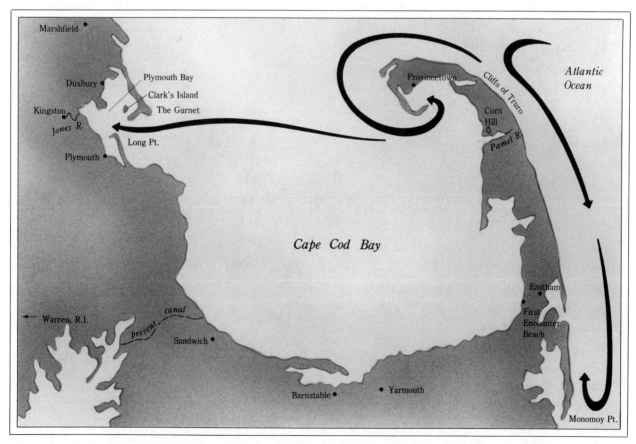

Arrows show the Mayflower's *approach of Cape Cod, near wreck off Monomoy Point, return to Provincetown, and eventual journey to Plymouth Bay.*

morning, they sank the kettle in the pond and took off through the woods, where they got lost.

While puzzling their way out they received a surprise hunting lesson from the Indians, comic because no one was injured. A sapling with a concealed noose had been bent over and the ground was baited with acorns. Bradford, coming in the rear, triggered it and, as the sapling sprang upward, Bradford was suspended with his leg caught in the noose. Hopkins, the only passenger who had previously been in America, explained that it was an Indian deer trap.

On nearing the *Mayflower* they shot off muskets, and the longboat shoved off to fetch them. Governor Carver and Captain Jones and many others came ashore to greet them with relief and delight; for, said Bradford, the Pilgrims "were marvellously glad and their hearts encouraged" by what Standish and his volunteers called "Our First Discovery."

There was, though, an ominous aspect to their discoveries.

Bradford observed that they could neither go nor come from the shore except at high water. "Oftentimes they waded to the middle of the thigh." Some did it of necessity, some for the pleasure of getting to stand ashore on firm land. "But," said Bradford, "it brought to the most, if not to all, coughs and colds (the weather proving suddenly cold and stormy) which afterwards turned to the scurvy, whereof many died."

Although the carpenters estimated that it would take two additional days to complete restoring the shallop, the Pilgrims decided to shove off November 27 for further exploration of the Pamet River area. "Our Second Discovery," as the Pilgrims called it, would cover four difficult days. Twenty-four men were picked to go, a number increased to thirty-four when Captain Jones expressed a wish to go, too, and brought nine of his crew.

Jones, in gratitude for his kindness, was chosen leader. They used both the shallop and the longboat. Confronted with "rough weather and cross winds," they were soon forced to seek the nearest shore "and then to wade out above the knees." Some of the men, worried about the loss of time, marched six or seven miles farther. "It blowed

and did snow all that day and night, and froze withal." Thinking back days later on their frigid experience, they reported "Some of our people that are dead took the original of their death here."

Next day, the shallop rejoined them and they sailed to the south of the Pamet River. Understandably, they called it "Cold Harbour." They decided it was navigable only for boats, not ships. After they had plodded up steep hills and down into deep valleys through six inches of snow, their wearied captain felt they should rest. Some wanted to explore farther, but made rendezvous for the night "under a few pine trees."

They had eaten little that day and dined "with soldiers' stomachs" when they bagged three fat geese and six ducks.

By morning they decided the land was too hilly and the harbor too shallow for a settlement and went looking for the place where they had cached the rest of the corn. This spot was on a hill near the seashore overlooking Cold Harbour. They named it "Corn Hill," still its name. They had to dig with cutlasses and short swords a foot into the frozen ground, and thanked God they had made their "First Discovery"

The Mayflower's *shallop*

trip, for the ground was now hidden by snow and hard frozen.

Bradford, in his history, emphasized what "a special providence of God" that first corn discovery had been:

"They got seed to plant them corn the next year, or else they might have starved, for they had none nor any likelihood to get any till the season had been past, as the sequel did manifest."

They dug in other places and, in all, got about ten bushels of corn, two or three baskets of wheat, and a bag of beans. Then weatherwise Captain Jones saw that the sky portended foul weather and wished to go back aboard the ship. And they sent back all the corn and "our weakest people and some that were sick." This return left eighteen who hoped to find Indians with whom they were eager to trade.

Next day these Pilgrims followed trails throughout the woods, but found no Indians. On the way back they came upon graves, especially one that was "much bigger and longer than any we had yet seen." Presently, they made an astonishing discovery on opening it. Besides the bones of a child, they found those of a man whose "skull had fine yellow hair still on it."

They tried to guess the mystery surely surrounding this burial. From seagoing articles in his grave, they concluded that the blond man was most likely to be another of the French sailors killed by the Nauset Indians after they were shipwrecked on Cape Cod back in 1616 and 1617.

In the late afternoon they discovered two Indian houses—arborlike lodges with roofs made from saplings that had been curved and covered with mats. Still, they found no Indians.

With night coming they hastened aboard the shallop and headed back to the *Mayflower*. They soon found that "cold and wet lodging had so tainted our people, for scarce any of us were free from vehement coughs."

Aboard ship, worried debate followed—lengthy despite the pressure for a speedy decision—on where they should settle. No place that they had yet explored seemed to satisfy their desire that the site should possess a good water supply, ample corn ground, a convenient harbor, good fishing, and that it be "healthful, secure and defensible."

The discussion was presently joined by a crewman who had an attractive suggestion.

The *Mayflower's* second mate, Robert Coppin, pilot of the *Speedwell*, recalled that on a voyage to the New World in 1614 he had seen a "good harbor" near another headland of Cape Cod. It was "some eight leagues (about twenty-four miles) distant," he told them; and, because an Indian there had made off with a harpoon during the trading, Coppin and his mates had called the place "Thievish Harbor."

The Pilgrims thereupon decided on a "Third Discovery" search, but not to go beyond "Thievish Harbor."

They were about to commence the first full week in December. It would be one of the most momentous in their voyage, with the weather, at times, brutal.

The affliction that Bradford would call the General Sickness now began to take its toll. On Monday, December 4, a young servant boy, Edward Thompson, died. Two days later another boy, Jasper More, died, one of four More children among the London orphans brought with the Pilgrims.

The weather on December 5 was "too foul" for the shallop to navigate. During the day the *Mayflower*, as told in *Mourt's Relation*, narrowly escaped possible destruction by gunpowder. One of the young sons of the colony's worst troublemaker, John Billington of London, found gunpowder and, in his father's absence, made "squibs" (firecrackers). More seriously, he discharged his father's fowling piece amid scattered gunpowder in the cabin, "there being a little barrel of powder half full . . . and yet, by God's mercy, no harm done."

The shallop set sail December 6. Among the eighteen volunteers were the foremost Pilgrims, including Governor Carver, William Bradford, Edward Winslow, and Myles Standish. Two of the Pilgrims' hired seamen were also along and six of the ship's crew, including First Mate John Clarke, who had made two prior voyages to America, and Mate Robert Coppin to show the way to Thievish Harbor.

The weather was "very cold and hard." It was some time before they could even get clear of Long Point. "The water froze on our clothes and made them many times like coats of iron."

After they got under the weather shore, however, the sailing was better and they went several leagues along the shore. As they landed at the present Eastham, they saw ten or twelve Indians cutting up a stranded grampus two or three miles away. The Pilgrims made a barricado and a fire and set sentinels. They could see the smoke from the Indians' fire that night a few miles away.

On the following day the company divided, some sailing along the shore and some exploring by land. In searches in the woods they found more graves and former Indian dwellings, but no Indians. They signaled the shallop as the sun began to draw low. "Weary and faint—for we had eaten nothing all that day," they prepared their camp—another barricado of logs, stakes, and thick pine boughs near the north bank where the present Herring River enters the bay.

Just about midnight they heard "a great and hideous cry; and our sentinels called, 'Arm! Arm!'" They shot off a couple of muskets and the noise ceased. "We concluded," they wrote, "that it was a company of wolves and foxes."

The next day, December 8, was to be one of their most exhausting and dangerous. The weather was the worst of the week, and that night the shallop was almost cast away, which would have meant, as they phrased it, "the overthrow of all."

As daybreak came they faced their first shock.

They started stirring about 5 A.M., held prayer, began preparing breakfast and moving things down to the shallop. Some went about moving down their armor, corselets, and guns, and four kept theirs—fortunately. As the others returned from the shallop to breakfast they heard again, as at midnight, "a great and strange cry," and one of the company came running in and yelling: "They are men! Indians! Indians!"

Thereupon, "arrows came flying amongst us."

The four Pilgrims with arms manned the open side of the barricado. Standish, who had a quick-firing snaphance (musket with flintlock), fired and so too did another. The other two held fire to be sure of targets. The men at the shallop fired three of their slower-firing matchlocks.

The Indians, not "less than thirty or forty," fled—after some had come daringly near to shoot

their arrows. The Pilgrims followed them for a quarter of a mile and fired a couple of muskets "that they might see we were not afraid."

None of the Pilgrims was injured. But for settlers, eager to meet and trade with their neighbors, the experience appeared deeply dismaying. Bradford said he later learned that the Indians conceived that the Pilgrims were confreres who had "come to revenge" the shipwrecked French sailors that tribe members among these Nauset Indians had murdered.

The Pilgrims retrieved their arrow-pierced coats from the barricado and gathered eighteen arrows that Captain Jones would later take back to England. The Pilgrims called the place "First Encounter Beach," still its name.

Coppin's estimate of the distance to his Thievish Harbor was more accurate than he realized, had the Pilgrim shallop gone directly westward across Cape Cod Bay. The shallop, however, had been sailing a route more than three times longer, the explorers keeping close to the coast of the bay so that they could spot any harbor.

The wind was good as they left First Encounter beach. For many miles they found "neither river nor creek." Then, after a couple of hours, the weather changed to snow and rain and in the afternoon the wind increased, "the seas began to be very rough . . . and the hinges of the rudder broke."

Two sailors struggled to steer with two oars. The seas "had grown so great that we were much troubled and in great danger; and the night grew on."

Their crisis soon intensified.

"Master Coppin bade us be of good cheer; he saw the harbour."

His shipmates, said Bradford, crowded on what sail they could "to get in while they could see. But herewith they broke their mast in three pieces and their sail fell overboard in a very grown sea, so as they had like to have been cast away. Yet, by God's mercy they recovered themselves, and having the flood [tide] with them, struck into the harbor."

Then came the worst moment:

Coppin, perceiving that ahead was "a cove full of breakers," cried out: "lord be merciful unto them for his eyes never saw that place before. . . ."

Apparently, instead of heading into Plymouth

Bay, they were being swept, with the tide and wind behind them, toward a beach between the Gurnet and Saguish Head.

Disaster was suddenly averted when one of the mariners—Bradford described him only as "a lusty sailor which steered,"—yelled to those rowing:

"About with her or else they were all cast away, the which they did with speed."

"So he bid them be of good cheer and row lustily, for there was a fair sound before them, and he doubted not but they should find one place or another where they might ride in safety. And though it was very dark and rained sore, yet in the end they got under the lee of a small island. . . ."

They would not know until morning that they had found safety on an island. The lusty sailor had brought them around Saquish Head to a small island just to its north in the future Duxbury Bay. Miraculously, he had also averted the shallop's striking another hazard at the entrance to Plymouth Bay, a shoal on which Samuel de Champlain's ship had grounded in 1605.

Mindful of what happened to them that morning at First Encounter beach, some of the Pilgrims considered it best to stay with the boat and keep watch. Others, also wet and cold, wanted to go ashore and make a fire. Some did, and when after midnight the wind shifted to the northwest "and it froze hard" the rest joined them.

The Pilgrims held their first Sabbath service on Clark's Island in the future Duxbury Bay while exploring the Plymouth area.

The morning brought a "fair, sunshining day." Marching around revealed they were on an island with "no inhabitants at all." They named it for First Mate Clarke, who had been the first to go ashore.

They proceeded comfortably to "dry their stuff, fix their pieces [weapons] and rest themselves; and gave God thanks for His mercies in their manifold deliverances." Thus they spent Saturday; and on the following day, the Sabbath, they rested.

On December 11, the next day, they explored Plymouth Bay and the shore and decided that here was "the best they could find, and the season and their present necessity made them glad to accept it."

They had first sounded the harbor and found it "fit for shipping." They had "marched into the land and found divers cornfields, and little running brooks, a place very good for situation." This had been the seat of the Patuxets, Squanto's people, who were wiped out by the plague. This was the place, Bradford learned later, where Captain Thomas Dermer had explored in 1619 and written back to Sir Ferdinando Gorges of his hope that here would be the first New England plantation.

"The Pilgrim leaders sailed twenty-five miles directly east back to the *Mayflower* and told the others about their exciting discovery, which, said Bradford, "did much comfort their hearts."

For Bradford, himself, however, there was dreadful news. His wife Dorothy—whom he had married in Holland in 1613 when she had just turned sixteen and who was mother of their five-year-old son John who had, like some other Pilgrim children, been left with Rev. John Robinson—was dead.

Rev. Cotton Mather, in an early account of Bradford's life, said Bradford's "dearest consort, accidentally falling overboard, was drowned in the harbour." This was on December 7, just a week after the seventh anniversary of their marriage, and just a day after Bradford had left the *Mayflower* to join in the perilous but decisive Third Discovery that led the Pilgrims to Plymouth.

Samoset's
Indian Greeting

S ome happy moments came to those aboard the *Mayflower* while the shallop was away on a Third Discovery trip. *Mourt's Relation* records how "it pleased God that Mistress White was brought to bed of a son, which was called Peregrine." Susanna White's new son, whose older brother was born at Leyden, was the first English child born in New England.

But mostly, the waiting, anxious hours for the *Mayflower* passengers were not happy.

"Dorothy Bradford was followed in death the next day by a victim of the General Sickness, a fifty-seven-year-old tailor recruited by the London adventurers. Many aboard were sick. The number of passengers would be steadily diminished. The General Sickness, within a few weeks, would take the lives of both Peregrine's father and the tailor's wife.

Indeed, when the passengers set about discussing where they should dwell, they had already dug four graves. A memorial to these departed Pilgrims, whose adventure into the New World in search of religious freedom and a new life had come so quickly to an end, may be seen at the center of Provincetown. And soon the dwindling band of pioneers would have many, many more untimely graves.

On December 15 Captain Jones weighed anchor and the *Mayflower* left Cape Cod Harbor. When the ship came within six miles of the future Plymouth Bay the headwinds made it distressingly impossible to "fetch the harbor," and she went back. With a fair wind the next day the Pilgrims put to sea again and managed to reach Plymouth Harbor safely just before the winds, which had shifted, could have again driven them back to Cape Cod.

Captain Jones dropped anchor just inside Beach Point, northern tip of the three-mile-long spit of land now called Plymouth Beach, which forms an eastern barrier and natural breakwater for Plymouth Harbor. The

Mayflower was "a mile and almost a half" from the granite boulder years later christened Plymouth Rock, an almost solitary glacier-age deposit on this part of the sandy and shallow shore.

The Pilgrims had arrived on Saturday, a time for preparing food, attire, and furnishings for the coming Sabbath that, regardless of lost time, they persisted in reverently observing as an occasion for religion and rest.

Still, they noticed from shipboard that the harbor was "a bay greater than Cape Cod" harbor and "compassed with goodly land." Stretching from their anchorage toward the future Kingston and Duxbury, the bay seemed to them "in fashion like a sickle or fish-hook."

No one went ashore until Monday, December 18. On that morning the Pilgrims initiated explorations ashore to decide exactly where on that sickle-shaped bay they would begin building. The search would consume three days. It began with Captain Jones and three or four sailors taking a group of Pilgrims to the shore.

For hours they marched along the coast and went seven or eight miles in the woods without seeing Indians. They examined land formerly planted by the Indians, its soil good to a "spit's [spade's] depth." They found a great variety of familiar trees and vines, "and many others which we know not." They found brooks and springs, and praised the water as "the best . . . that ever was drunk." Weary from marching, they went back that night to the *Mayflower*.

Some by land and some in the shallop pressed their search the next day. The shallop went three miles up a creek in the future town of Kingston and the Pilgrims named the present Jones River after the *Mayflower*'s captain. They also crossed the bay to examine Clark's Island.

On returning that night to the *Mayflower* they resolved that the next day they would "settle on some of those places" they had just seen.

In the morning they "called on God for direction" and went for "a better view" of just two of the places previously explored. Clark's Island was excluded as simply too small. They felt keenly the need to save time, "our victuals being much spent, especially our beer." And so, immediately after an additional look,

The Pilgrims' first step on Plymouth Rock is depicted in Landing of the Pilgrims, *by Henry A. Bacon.*

they voted for the high ground they had inspected on the first day—the land back of the great rock.

Here was everything they sought. They reported:

"There is a great deal of land cleared, and hath been planted with corn three or four years ago; and there is a very sweet brook runs under the hill-side, and many delicate springs . . . and where we may harbour our shallops and boats exceedingly well; and in this brook such good fish in their seasons; on the further side of the river also much corn-ground cleared. In one field is a great hill, on which we point to make a platform and plant our ordnance. . . ."

Thus, before names had been bestowed on them, the Pilgrims were describing Cole's Hill, directly back of Plymouth Rock; Town Brook on the hill's south side; Pilgrim Spring, still flowing in Brewster Garden; and, 165 feet above the sea, Burial Hill, on which they would build a fort and meetinghouse—a hill from which they could that day "see thence Cape Cod."

Twenty decided to spend the night right there, and those returning to the *Mayflower* promised to be back in the morning to start building houses.

Harsh December weather interfered. That night came a tempest of pelting rain and strong winds. The twenty men ashore had insufficient daylight remaining to build an adequate "court of guard" (protection) and were soaked. They "had no victuals on land," and the wind blew so fiercely that the shallop could not return. On the *Mayflower*, meanwhile, it was necessary to "ride with three anchors ahead."

The gale made travel next day between ship and shore impossible. On this day Mary, wife of Isaac Allerton, gave birth to a stillborn son. Mary, mother of three children born in Leyden, would herself die in a few weeks.

Preparations for building did get under way on Saturday, December 23, with as many as were able joining those ashore. First, though, they had to dig two graves, one for the stillborn Allerton infant and another for a youth from London who had died on shipboard on the first day of the storm.

On that Saturday and the following days, even on Christmas Day, they kept busy—"some to fell timber, some to saw, some to rive [split], and some to carry; so no man rested all that day." Bradford, moreover, wrote that it was on Christmas Day that they "began

to erect the first house for common use to receive them and their goods." The common house was atop Cole's Hill, on its south side, and near the foot of the present Leyden Street, the first street in New England.

That Christmas night on the *Mayflower* Captain Jones provided "some beer, but on shore none at all."

Most days during the rest of December brought foul weather, leaving the people ashore "much troubled and discouraged." On December 28 the Pilgrims made a very practical decision, after concluding that "two rows of houses and a fair street" along with a platform for ordnance on the hilltop would be "easier impaled." The decision was to have single men without wives join families "so we might build fewer houses." Then lots were cast for nineteen household units.

The Pilgrims were already talking about "the weakness of our people." They recorded that many were "growing ill with colds; for our former discoveries in frost and storms, and the wading at Cape Cod had brought much weakness amongst us, which increased so every day more and more." By December's end six had died. In January eight more would follow them, and still the agony and the dreadful toll from the General Sickness would grow.

Keen as the Pilgrims were to become acquainted with their Indian neighbors, they worried that the reduction in their number might invite attack. To conceal their losses, they resorted to burials in unmarked graves on Cole's Hill.

Those doing the building saw, at a distance they judged to be six or seven miles, smoke from Indian fires. And on January 3, some who had gone to gather thatch, "saw great fires of the Indians," went to the former cornfields and yet saw no Indians. Next day Myles Standish and four or five others sought to meet the Indians. They found Indian dwellings "not lately inhabited"—but again no Indians.

As the twenty-foot-square common house neared completion, with about eight days more needed to finish the thatching, the Pilgrims on January 9 decided on a new plan for building their small, frame family houses. On that day they divided the meersteads (house lots) and garden plots "after the proportion formerly allotted," and agreed that "every many should build his own house, thinking by that course men would make more haste than working in common."

This sort of private initiative was a principle in which the Pilgrims, closeknit as they were in fellowship, deeply believed. Allegiance to it was their reason for refusing, when leaving Southampton, to accede to the harsh demands made by Thomas Weston and the London adventurers. They would adhere to this principle in the future in other crucial decisions about developing their plantation.

The January weather, however, was so foul that "seldom could we work half the week."

Pilgrims aboard the *Mayflower* were up early Sunday, January 14, to go to join those on land—by then a larger group—for their first Sabbath meeting ashore. The wind was blowing strongly, and as they looked toward Leyden Street they suddenly "espied their great new rendezvous on fire." A spark had landed on the thatch and the fire was rapidly spreading.

Bradford, three days earlier, while at work, had been stricken with such pain in hipbone and legs that there was fear he would die. He already had a severe cold from the explorations. When the thatch flared up Bradford as well as Governor Carver, who had just been leading a search party for two thatch gatherers lost in the woods, lay sick in bed in the common house. Near them were charged muskets and gunpowder. "Through God's mercy," relates *Mourt's Relation*, "they had no harm."

The fire consumed only the thatch. The roof still stood, but some who had transferred ashore had to resume quarters aboard the *Mayflower*.

The common house, however, had not provided adequate quarters. It had been "as full of beds as they could lie one by another." Besides repairing the roof, then the Pilgrims spent two days building a shed "to put our common provisions in."

They did get to keep their first Sabbath meeting ashore on the following Sunday, January 21. During the rest of the month, when "frosty weather and sleet" would let them, the Pilgrims used the shallop and longboat to bring ashore common provisions, like hogsheads of meal. These they carried up to storage.

The manifold tasks facing them were made more arduous by illness, on shipboard and ashore, and the steady decline in their numbers. Eight more of the *Mayflower* passengers died during January.

"The sickness," said Bradford, "began to fall sore amongst them" after the fire. In February the General Sickness would bring their greatest loss of life, with sometimes two or three buried in one night. In all, seventeen more of the passengers would perish by the end of February, and one of the small houses—briefly endangered when a spark kindled the roof—had to be pressed into use to help care for the increased number of those who were sick.

The February weather continued mostly severe after starting "with the greatest gusts of winds that ever we had since we came forth." The *Mayflower,* lightened now because of the goods that had been brought ashore, was "in danger." Often the weather made work impossible. And by mid-month the Pilgrims were deeply disturbed about their security.

One of the Pilgrims on February 16, a fair day, went fowling in the reeds about a mile and a half from the plantation. Suddenly he saw, passing him, a dozen Indians headed toward the plantation and he could hear in the woods "the noise of many more." He laid low, and then ran home to give the alarm.

On that same day Myles Standish and a companion left their tools in the woods and, on returning, found that the Indians had taken them.

Muskets that had been allowed to get out of temper (firing condition) because of moisture and rain were promptly put in order, and a strict watch was set. The next day, the Pilgrims assembled to establish "military orders among ourselves." Myles Standish was formally elected "our captain" and was voted full authority to command in military matters.

Even as they were engaged in this activity, two Indians appeared atop the much higher Watson's Hill (the Pilgrims called it Strawberry Hill) south of the plantation, immediately across Town Brook. Captain Standish and Stephen Hopkins hurried across the brook and laid down a musket to show their desire to parley. The Indians—with even more of them concealed behind the hill—abruptly took off.

The sudden appearance of so large a number of Indians and suspicion that many more were around set the puzzled Pilgrims to getting their ordnance placed.

Captain Jones, with some crewmen, brought ashore a minion—a cannon with a 3 1/4-inch bore. This, along with a cannon of larger bore called a saker,which had been left by the seashore, were lugged to the platform on top of Burial Hill. They were mounted there along with two smaller cannon called bases, which had a 1 1/4-inch bore. The work was completed on February 21—the same day on which four passengers died, among them the father of Peregrine White.

During March the General Sickness claimed thirteen more lives. Still, during this month the Pilgrims would for the first time hear thunder in New England, catch bird songs, and sow garden seeds—true signs all of springtime and renewed hope.

"The Spring now approaching," said Bradford, "it pleased God the mortality began to cease amongst them, and the sick and the lame recovered apace, which put as it were new life into them, though they had borne their sad affliction with much patience and contentedness as I think any people could do. But it was the Lord which upheld them. . . ."

When the General Sickness had finally run its course fully half the *Mayflower* passengers had perished.

The loss among the wives was the heaviest. Of the eighteen couples, eight of the men but only four of the women survived. Four families were wiped out, and in only three families did all the members survive. Six children lost one parent and five lost both parents.

Children, though, fared best, twenty-five of the thirty-two surviving. Of the eleven young women only one died. Among the nine young male servants the toll was appalling: all but one perished.

Two doctors were among them: the *Mayflower's* doctor, Giles Heale, and Deacon Fuller, a weaver while in Leyden, who functioned as the Pilgrims' "surgeon and physician." Fuller, said Bradford, was a tender-hearted man and "a great help and comfort to them." During the General Sickness, however, neither doctor was mentioned. Perhaps, like Bradford, they were among the stricken.

Accounts are far from specific as to the name or

The Mayflower on Her Arrival in Plymouth Harbor, *by William Formby Halsall*

proper treatment for the dreadful sickness. Medical techniques in that day were still so primitive that they could have brought more harm than cure to patients unquestionably suffering from improper diet, anxiety, overexertion and exposure to damp and cold. Bradford ascribed the affliction to "the scurvy and other diseases which this long voyage and their inac-comodate condition had brought upon them." The other diseases could have been pneumonia or ship's fever, a form of typhus.

Captain Jones and his crew did not escape. "Almost half of their company died before they went away," said Bradford, "many of their officers and lustiest men, as the boatswain, gunner, three quartermasters, the cook and others." Neither the names of the crew, beyond a few, nor their exact number have come down to us. Their estimated loss of life must be added to the steep figure we have of passengers' deaths.

Some of the crew were distinctly not so benevolent as the Pilgrims. Bradford tells how one of his fellow sufferers ashore sent word to the *Mayflower* that he desired "a small can of beer." A crewman callously responded "that if he were their own father he should have none." Captain Jones was mortified, and said that he would provide some beer even "though he drank water homeward bound."

Bradford also told of the "rare example" shown during the General Sickness by the six or seven Pilgrims who escaped the affliction. These, he said:

"Spared no pains night nor day, but with abundance of toil and hazard of their own health, fetched them [the sick] wood, made them fires, dressed them meat, made their beds, washed their loathsome clothes, clothed and unclothed them. In a word, did all the homely and necessary offices for them which dainty and queasy stomachs cannot endure to hear named. . . ."

"Two of these seven were Mr. William Brewster, their Reverend Elder, and Myles Standish, their Captain and military commander, unto whom myself and many others were much beholden in our low and sick condition."

From Leyden their beloved pastor, Rev. John Robinson, wrote in June: "The death of so many of our dear friends and brethren, oh! how grievous hath it been. . . ." He still was confident that God's mercy could be seen in that He had spared so many of the leaders and would give victory to their struggle to provide "godly and wise government."

Since coming to the New World, all the future builders of Plymouth, save Elder Brewster, had been widowed—Bradford by an accident, Winslow and Standish by the General Sickness. In their survival the Reverend Robinson wrote that he still foresaw triumph for all the hopes that rode with them when they left Delftshaven back in July to join the *Mayflower*.

Mid-March at last brought the beautiful greeting that the Pilgrims had hoped and long yearned to hear since they had first caught sight of the New England coast.

On March 16, Captain Standish and the adult men—now fewer than two dozen—were once again interrupted as they sought to complete discussing their new military organization. A tall, straight Indian, "stark naked, only a leather about his waist," carrying a bow and two arrows, caused an alarm as he approached the common house.

Further describing the Indian's sensational arrival, *Mourt's Relation* continued: "He very boldly came all alone, and along the houses, straight to the rendezvous. . . . He saluted us in English, and bade us, 'Welcome!' "

Peace Treaty
with Massasoit

The surprise visitor, an impressive figure of "seemly carriage," was Samoset, an Algonquin sagamore (chief) from Pemaquid Point in Maine.

The astounded Pilgrims did not invite him inside their rendezvous, the common house, lest they reveal their limited number. It was a fair, warm day and they questioned him until night was coming, for Samoset was the first native "we could meet withal." He was "free in speech," though somewhat difficult to understand because he spoke, said Bradford "in broken English."

Samoset had learned this tongue from sailors who had been coming for years to Monhegan Island, about ten miles off the Pemaquid Point coast, to fish and to trade. Samoset had come to the Plymouth area some eight months earlier with Captain Thomas Dermer.

Accustomed to English ways, Samoset asked for some beer. The Pilgrims had none, and instead they gave him some "strong water [liquor] . . . biscuit and butter and cheese and pudding and a piece of mallard." And when the wind began to rise a little, they solicitously "cast a horseman's coat about him."

Samoset had quite a bit to offer them. He recounted names of ships, captains, and mates who visited Monhegan, and gave details about the "east parts where he lived, which was afterwards profitable to them." And from Samoset the Pilgrims also, at last, received information about their Indian neighbors and about this place where they were busy constructing their dwellings.

Its Indian name was Accomack. The clearings that had been made for cornfields were those of the local Patuxet tribe, whose members had perished in the plague four years past. The nearest neighbors to the Pilgrims now were other Wampanoag Indians whose great sachem, Massasoit, lived forty miles inland at Sowans, in the present Warren, Rhode Island, on Narragansett Bay. Massasoit had 60 warriors and the Nausets on Cape Cod, who had escaped the plague, had 100—all "ill affected toward the English" since the villainous Captain Thomas Hunt, equally reviled in England, kidnapped "20 Patuxets out of this very place we inhabit and seven men from the Nausets . . . and sold them for slaves."

As night came, the Pilgrims, out of caution, would gladly have had Samoset leave, but he wanted to stay the night. The Pilgrims thought shipboard would be safest for them, and finding that he was willing, they went to the shallop. Winds had grown stronger and the shallop could not get back to the *Mayflower*. Samoset therefore was lodged in Stephen Hopkins's house; he was the only Pilgrim with prior knowledge of Indians. His house was directly across Leyden Street from Elder Brewster's.

With gifts of "a knife, a bracelet and a ring," Samoset departed next morning, first making a promise that must have been highly encouraging to the debt-laden Pilgrims, a promise that he would be

back again with some other Indians "with such beavers' skins as they had to truck."

The Indians, of course, had quite naturally been watching these newcomers, probably from the time they first dropped anchor off the coast. Recently, Bradford observed, the Indians had been coming closer and even deliberately revealing their presence. This wary reconnaissance was now approaching a dramatic climax.

Samoset was back next day, a Sunday, with "five other, tall, proper men." As the Pilgrims had arranged with them, the Indians left their bows and arrows a quarter mile from the town. Some wore deer's skins, some wild cat's skins or fox tail, and some "had their faces painted black, from forehead to the chin, four or five fingers broad."

"We gave them entertainment as we thought was fitting them," continued *Mourt's Relation*, "They did eat liberally of our English victuals. They made semblance unto us of friendship and unity." Indeed, they brought back the tools that Captain Standish had missed a month ago in the woods. And, said *Mourt's*

Thanksgiving with Indians, *by N. C. Wyeth, shows a Pilgrim maid serving food to Indians, who were frequent visitors to Plymouth Colony.*

Relation, "they sang and danced after their manner, like antics."

Samoset and his friends had brought along, as he had promised, some beaver skins. But eager as the Pilgrims were to initiate trade, they still would not barter on the Sabbath. In fact, because of the day's obligations, they were eager for the Indians to depart. They did urge the Indians to come again and bring more skins "and we would truck for all." Each Indian was given a gift—"some trifles," but then it developed that Samoset wanted to stay. The rest took off.

Samoset "either was sick or feigned himself so," said the Pilgrims. The Indian, it appeared, was merely trying to see what further he might learn about these Europeans. He stayed the first days in the week, which were so fair and warm that the Pilgrims dug ground and planted more garden seed. These were British seeds, wheat and peas, and some of them, said Bradford, "came not to good," having become defective.

At this midweek, on March 21, the *Mayflower* voyage came finally to an end for the last of the passengers. The carpenter, recovered from scurvy, completed some repairs to the shallop, and it went "to fetch all from aboard." Their names have not come down to us but among them could have been some who, like the crew, had had the *Mayflower* for a home since it left London back in July.

On this day Samoset departed. The Pilgrims gave him some English clothing—hat, shoes, stockings, and shirt—and, showing their eagerness to trade, asked him to learn from his companions why they had not returned "to truck."

With Samoset gone, the Pilgrims once again resumed discussion on their military organization. They had talked only an hour when they were again interrupted, this time by two or three Indians—"daring us, as we thought—who appeared on Watson's Hill just across Town Brook. Captain Standish and a companion, with muskets, ran toward them, but as the Pilgrims drew near, the Indians "made show of defiance" and fled. Or did it mean something else?

March 22, the next day—"a very fair, warm day"—would be one of the most important in the plantation's entire life.

Again the men assembled to discuss their public business. And again, they had been scarcely an hour together when Samoset returned. With him was the only remaining native of Patuxet, Squanto, one of the Indians kidnapped by the notorious Captain Hunt. Having lived in England, Squanto, as Samoset had told them, could speak better England than himself. The Indians had "some few skins to truck and some red herrings, newly taken and dried, but not salted."

They also had sensational news:

"Their great sagamore, Massasoit, was hard by, with Quadequina, his brother, and all their men!"

Samoset and Squanto could not have been far ahead of the Indian chief and his entourage—his warriors, and "their wives and their women"—for hardly an hour had passed before "the king came to the top of the hill over against us, and had in his train sixty men, that we could well behold them, and they us."

The sight atop Watson's Hill was spectacular. Massasoit's attire differed little from that of his warriors save that he had "a great chain of white bone beads about his neck." His face was painted "a sad

Statue of Massasoit on Cole's Hill, Plymouth

red, like murrey [mulberry]." In Indian fashion, he was "oiled both head and face. . . . All his followers likewise were in their faces, in part or in whole, painted, some black, some red, some yellow, and some white . . . some had skins on them, and some naked; all strong, tall men in appearance."

The Pilgrims, looking at the warrior array, could readily see that the Indians outnumbered them nearly three to one. On their part, the Pilgrims sought also to be as impressive as their resources would permit.

Both Pilgrims and Indians were wary. When neither group gave sign of sending its leader, Squanto went across the brook and returned with word that Massasoit desired that "we should send one to parley with him." The choice for this crucial diplomatic task was Edward Winslow—twenty-five years of age, courageous, innovative, Elder Brewster's sturdy right arm, a future governor of Plymouth Plantation.

Winslow brought as gifts a pair of knives and a copper chain with a jewel in it for Massasoit, likewise a knife and "a jewel to hang in his ear" for Quadequina; and "a pot of strong water, a good quantity of biscuit and some butter."

Though Pilgrim Winslow was hardly on speaking terms with the king of England, Winslow began his speech to Massasoit with the assurance "that King James saluted him with words of love and peace, and did accept of him as his friend and ally; and that our governor desired to see him and to truck with him and to confirm a peace with him as his next neighbor."

The Pilgrim food furnished a hilltop repast, and Massasoit was much taken with Winslow's sword and armor. Winslow then remained as hostage with the sachem's brother while Massasoit and twenty of his warriors crossed the brook. They did leave their bows and arrows behind, though the sachem kept "in his bosom, hanging in a string, a great long knife." Six or seven of the warriors became hostages for Winslow.

Massasoit was met by Captain Standish, an aide, and six musketeers. After exchanging salutes, he was taken to a house then being built in which the Pilgrims had placed a green rug and three or four cushions for their visitor. Governor Carver immediately entered, to the sound of drum and trumpet. Behind him came a few musketeers.

There were official salutations. Governor Carver kissed Massasoit's hand, Massasoit responded in kind, and they sat down. When the Governor called for strong water and drank to him, Massasoit in turn took "a great draught that made him sweat all the while after." They ate a little fresh meat; and thereupon concluded a six-point treaty that the Pilgrims assured Massasoit would make King James "esteem of him as his friend and ally."

The Pilgrims then conducted Massasoit back to the brook. There, instead of receiving Winslow, they were greeted by Massasoit's brother. Quadequina—"a very proper, tall young man of a very modest and seemly countenance,"—was also well entertained. On Quadequina's return to the brook, the Indians released their hostage, Winslow.

The peace treaty was expressed in simple, direct words:

Neither people was to harm the other. Each would punish their own offenders against the other's people. If anything was stolen, it would be returned. Each would aid the other in the event "any did unjustly war against him." Each would seek to have the other's "neighbor confederates" join in the treaty. Each would leave any weapons at a distance when making visits.

That night Massasoit and his men camped in the woods a half mile away. Only Samoset and Squanto stayed with the Pilgrims, "who kept good watch" but found "no appearances of danger." Massasoit and his people departed the next morning, leaving behind a promise they would come again.

The treaty, now mutually confirmed, offered a prospect with peace and security for the religious haven the Pilgrims were creating. In fact, they felt that the treaty could be decisive as to whether or not the plantation would have a future here at all. And as events turned out, the treaty made it possible to fulfill other pressing needs of the Pilgrim settlers: an adequate food supply, and development of trade so that the Pilgrims could free themselves from Old World debt.

At the moment, though, the Pilgrims had no way of knowing whether this farreaching treaty would last. Massasoit had hardly taken his leave, after giving some groundnuts and tobacco to Captain Standish and Isaac Allerton, when the Pilgrims started speculating on Massasoit's motivation for making the treaty.

They could not "conceive but that he is willing to have peace with us" because Indians had had numerous opportunities to injure Pilgrims working or fowling in the woods and yet "offered them no harm." The Pilgrims had also observed that Massasoit "trembled for fear" while seated with the governor, and that his brother, Quadequina, had made "signs of dislike" until Pilgrim weaponry was removed. "Our pieces," they said, "are terrible unto them."

Above all, the Pilgrims had learned of an Indian menace confronting Massasoit. It came from the powerful tribe that lived on the west side of Narragansett Bay—a tribe that had sustained no losses from the dreadful pestilence back in 1616-1617. Massasoit, concluded the Pilgrims:

"hath a potent adversary, the Narragansetts, that are at war with him, against whom he thinks we may be some strength to him." They would be—and very soon.

That Friday, March 23, was an important day at Plymouth. Squanto, following up his vital contribution as interpreter-diplomat during Massasoit's visit, launched on his role as instructor to the Pilgrims, a service that would lead a grateful Bradford to describe Squanto as "a special instrument sent by God for their good beyond their expectation." That spring, Squanto, said Bradford:

"Directed them how to set their corn, where to take fish, and to procure other commodities, and was also their pilot to bring them to unknown places for their profit, and never left them till he died."

Right after Massasoit departed, Squanto showed the Pilgrims how to catch eels. Presumably he went to the stream just south of Plymouth Harbor, the one now called Eel River. "He trod them out with his feet, and so caught them with his hands, without any other instrument." The eels were "fat and sweet," and everyone felt glad when Squanto came back that night "with as many as he could well lift in one hand."

Meanwhile Captain Standish, in a session so often interrupted, finally completed the Pilgrims' military

Treaty with Massasoit, by Henry Botkin, depicts Governor Carver and Massasoit making a peace agreement, the terms of which were kept for many decades.

arrangements. With March 25, their New Year's Day under the old style, only two days away, the Pilgrims proceeded to hold an election and again chose John Carver as their governor. Carver, like Elder Brewster, was in his mid-fifties; the oldest of the surviving Pilgrims, he had but a few weeks of life remaining.

Some laws were also adopted that Friday that were most timely. Soon thereafter a lawful order by Captain Standish brought a torrent of abuse from one of the Londoners, John Billington, whose violent nature would steer him eventually to the gallows. As punishment Billington had "his neck and heels tied together." His humble plea for pardon brought this first offender in the colony a quick, compassionate release, but produced no reform in Billington.

April 5 was finally chosen as the day for the *Mayflower* to begin its return voyage. As the day came not one Pilgrim, despite the suffering, hardship, and death that had been their lot since coming to the New World, gave the slightest sign of wishing to go back with the surviving crew.

Bradford went to unusual length in explaining the ship's delayed departure:

"The reason on their [the Pilgrims'] part why she stayed so long, was the necessity and danger that lay upon them; for it was well toward the end of December before she could land anything here, or they able to receive anything ashore. Afterwards, the 14th of January, the house which they had made for the general rendezvous by casualty fell afire, and some were fain to retire aboard for shelter, then the sickness began to fall sore amongst them, and the weather so bad they could not make much sooner any dispatch.

"Again the governor and chief among them, seeing so many die and fall down sick daily, thought it no wisdom to send away the ship, their condition considered and the danger they stood in from the Indians, till they could procure some shelter; and therefore thought it better to draw some more charge [debt] upon themselves and friends than hazard all.

"The master and the seamen likewise, though before they hasted the passengers ashore to be gone, now many of their men being dead . . . and the rest many lay sick and weak; the master durst not put to sea till he saw his men begin to recover, and the heart of the winter over."

For Captain Jones the *Mayflower's* return would be his last. Like so many of his unknown crew, he may have "taken the original" of his death in the exposure and strain that contributed to the General Sickness. The *Mayflower* reached London in roughly a month, on May 6, a quick passage. But in just a few months more Captain Jones's widow and their two children buried him in the churchyard in Rotherhithe on the south bank of the Thames River.

In The Return of the *Mayflower (N. C. Wyeth), Pilgrims watch as the* Mayflower, *their sole link to the Old World, drops below the horizon.*

A Hearty
First Thanksgiving

W̲ith spring came time for planting the main crop. The Pilgrims got out the seed corn they had taken in mid-November from Corn Hill—the corn without which, Bradford recorded, "they might have starved."

To help with this strange seed Squanto was providentially at hand, showing them "how to set it, and after how to dress and tend it. Also he told them, except they got fish and set with it in these old grounds it would come to nothing."

The fish were herring that in springtime, around mid-April, swim up Town Brook to spawn. Squanto showed the Pilgrims how to trap a store of these herrings and how to plant the corn in little mounds above the herring. He also instructed them to guard the mounds to ward off wolves and other predators attracted by the decaying herring as it provided fertilizer to the corn.

While the tilling and planting were under way, Governor Carver, suddenly stricken ill, came home from the cornfields. In a few hours he fell into a coma, and within a few days he passed away. He had been among the hardest workers and this fact, the lamenting Pilgrims felt certain, had "shortened his days." In little more than a month his wife, too, passed away. They had no children.

At the time of Carver's death Bradford had not yet recovered from his own illness. Nevertheless, the Pilgrims chose the thirty-one-year-old Bradford, as Rev. Cotton Mather of the Puritans later expressed it, to be "the leader of a people in a wilderness." The difficulties then facing Bradford were so many, said Cotton, "had he not been a person of more than ordinary piety, wisdom and courage, he must have sunk under them." Bradford's illness had taken him "near the point of death," and so the Pilgrims also elected an assistant, Isaac Allerton, to help him.

With springtime and renewed hopes, romance also came to new Plymouth. The first English child born in New England, Peregrine White, and his brother, got a new home when their mother on May 12 became the bride of Edward Winslow in New England's first English marriage ceremony. Both had lost their mates in the General Sickness. Winslow's adherence to their Dutch-style civil marriage on that May day would lead to his being harshly imprisoned by Archbishop Laud while on a later diplomatic journey to England for the colony.

Winslow had a major part in one of Bradford's earliest efforts as governor. In July, Bradford initiated journeys into the countryside that were planned to help the Pilgrims learn about their Indian neighbors and the wilderness. Several trips followed in that summer and fall, one of them a rescue mission to the Cape. All were filled with the dangers and exciting wonders in exploring unknown terrain and encountering strangers.

Winslow set out July 3 on a five-day trip to Sowans, the seat of Massasoit forty miles away. With him

New England's First Marriage, *by Paul Hawthorne, shows Edward Winslow and widow Susanna White being united.*

was the experienced Stephen Hopkins and Squanto as guide and interpreter. The mission had several objectives besides the desire "to continue the league of peace and friendship between them and us." The group was to "discover the country . . . as also to see their strength."

They had still another vital objective. Ever since Massasoit came to Plymouth his Indian subjects had come in quite a flow to see the plantation, eat, and invite gifts. The Pilgrims, uncertain about their food supply, felt they must cut down this liberal entertainment, they hoped without giving offense, "not knowing how our corn might prosper." It was a touchy assignment for any diplomat.

Indians all along the group's route to Narragansett Bay, particularly at Namasket [Middleborough] were kindly, helping the Pilgrims to ford streams and sharing their repasts of corn bread, fish, and boiled acorns. One of the Pilgrims profoundly impressed the Indians at Namasket by shooting, from fourscore paces, a crow that was damaging their corn.

The Pilgrims got a hearty welcome from Massasoit on reaching Sowans on July 8. He took them to his house and put on a gift Winslow had brought him: "a horeseman's coat of red cotton and laced with a slight lace." Massasoit was "not a little proud," and so too were his warriors "to see their king so bravely attired."

On hearing the Pilgrims' appeal, Massasoit at once assented to every request. He would stop the flood of visitors. Any messenger from him would wear the copper-chain identification Winslow had also brought and, as overlord of the Nausets, Massasoit would help the Pilgrims in seeking to make payment for the seed corn they had taken at Corn Hill. Furthermore, he gave them some of his seed corn, so that the Pilgrims could decide which produced better on their soil at Plymouth.

Massasoit had come "so newly home" he had no victuals to offer them. As it grew late he did invite them to use his bed, they at one end, and he and his wife at the other. The bed was "only planks laid a foot from the ground and a thin mat upon them." Two of Massasoit's chief warriors who dropped in were also invited to find space for themselves on the bed. The effect on the Pilgrims was "that we were worse weary of our lodging than of our journey."

There were games in the morning and some target shooting by the Pilgrims. In early afternoon the Indians brought two big fish and boiled them for "at least forty" to share. Massasoit pressed his visitors to stay longer, but they said they were eager to get back for the Sabbath.

The Pilgrims had feared that they might be "light-headed for want of sleep, for what with bad lodging, the savages' barbarous singing (for they use to sing themselves asleep), lice and fleas within doors, and mosquitoes without, we could hardly sleep all the time our being there; we much fearing that if we should stay any longer, we should not be able to recover home to want of strength."

They left Friday morning before sunrise. Massasoit in parting told through Squanto that he was "grieved and ashamed he could no better entertain them." He did send Squanto on a round of his subject tribes to try to furnish skins for trading with the Pilgrims, and provided them another Indian to be their guide. En route home, they were well received by Indians and especially at Namasket, where, "it pleased God to give them good store of fish, so that we were well refreshed."

Statue of Governor William Bradford at Plymouth Harbor

Bradford was particularly impressed by Winslow's report that, while the hostile Narragansetts, living across the bay from Massasoit and untouched by the plague, "were a strong people and many in number," there had been shocking signs of the plague's devastating effect on the Wampanoags.

Thousands had died. "They had not been able to bury one another," said Bradford: "their skulls and bones were found in many places lying still above the ground where their houses and dwellings had been, a very sad spectacle to behold."

Early in August Governor Bradford, with ten armed men and Squanto as guide, took the shallop on a three-day rescue mission to the Cape when the colonists were once again distressed by one of the Billington youngsters. This time it was not firecrackers. It was that young John Billington had got lost in the woods. Bradford had sought Massasoit's help, and the sachem, through his messengers, was able to report that John was in the hands of the Nauset Indians.

The trip, through Massasoit's intercession, was highly successful, though beclouded near the end by a false report that Massasoit had been captured by the Narragansetts.

On the way to the Nausets the Pilgrims anchored in Barnstable Harbor and were graciously entertained by the chief at Cummaquid, an Indian village, with his men singing, dancing, and sharing their feast of lobsters and fish. It was these Indians who had found young John, who had been living on berries, and had sent him to the chief of the Nausets, Aspinet, whose warriors had attacked the Pilgrims at First Encounter Beach.

A pathetic sight at Cummaquid was "the weeping and crying" of a woman "no less than a hundred years old." The Pilgrims, grieved by her sorrow, asked the reason and were told that three of her sons had been kidnapped by villainous Captain Hunt, the same who kidnapped Squanto. This outrage had deprived her of "the comfort of her children in her old age."

The Pilgrims told her that all the English condemned Hunt and gave her some gifts.

When the Pilgrims arrived at First Encounter Beach and the boat was aground Bradford satisfied the Nausets, who were swarming around them, for the corn taken from Corn Hill, and exchanged promises of trade with them.

Aspinet appeared after sunset with a great train of warriors and one carrying the Billington boy through the water toward the boat. Aspinet "had no less than a hundred with him, the half whereof came to the shallop side unarmed with him, the other half stood aloof with their bows and arrows. There he delivered us the boy, behung with beads, and made peace with us; we bestowing a knife on him, and likewise on another that first encountered the boy and brought him thither. So they departed from us."

Hunting Wild Turkey, *by N. C. Wyeth, depicts Pilgrims and Indians joining in the harvest hunt.*

During this exchange the Pilgrims picked up word that Massasoit had been taken. "This," said Bradford, "struck some fear in us, because the colony was so weakly guarded, the strength thereof being abroad. But we set forth with resolution to make the best haste home we could."

On their return home, which was delayed by weather, Squanto and Hobomok, another friendly Indian who had come to live at Plymouth, went to Namasket to see what they could learn about Massasoit. There they were set upon by a deceitful follower of the Wampanoag sachem, Corbitant, possibly jealous of these two Indians' rapport with the Pilgrims.

Hobomok, a strong man, broke free and rushed back to Plymouth to tell of his fear that Squanto had been slain. The last he had seen of Squanto was with Corbitant holding "a knife to his breast."

The Pilgrims resolved on immediate action. Bradford dispatched Captain Standish and some dozen armed men with Hobomok as guide. Their orders were: "If they found that Squanto was killed, to cut off Corbitant's head."

In the night-time assault on Corbitant's house a couple of Indians were slightly injured. But Captain Standish found that Corbitant had fled and Squanto was safe. Corbitant had only made a threat to kill

him. Hobomok explained to the Namasket Indians that the intended quarry was strictly Corbitant, and so the Indians ceased trembling and all shared some food. The two wounded Indians were brought back for Deacon Fuller to dress their wounds and were then sent home.

"Much firmer peace" was the outcome.

The Pilgrims soon possessed a document dated September 13, 1621, on which seven Indian chiefs had placed their names or a mark. Winslow, writing about it to Bradford's brother-in-law in England, George Morton—probably the Mourt of *Mourt's Relation*—told of improved security in the plantation:

"It hath pleased God so to possess the Indians with a fear of us and love unto us, that not only the greatest king amongst them, called Massasoit, but also all the princes and peoples round about us, have either made suit unto us, or been glad of any occasion to make peace with us; so that seven of them at once have sent their messengers to us to that end. Yea, an isle at sea, which we never saw, hath also, together with the former, yielded willingly to be under the protection and subject to our sovereign lord King James."

The isle at sea was called Capawack by the Indians, our Martha's Vineyard. On that September 13 document were names or marks representing the Indian leaders to the south and west of New Plymouth. Even Corbitant, with Massasoit mediating, got himself included. Bradford next sought information, peace, and trade with the Indians north of Plymouth, the Massachusetts tribe around the future Boston Harbor.

On September 18, as midnight approached, Bradford picked ten men, headed by Captain Standish, with Squanto as interpreter and two other Indians, to go in the shallop on this four-day mission. Two more chiefs would sign, bringing to nine the total on the Pilgrims' peace list. Each, like Massasoit, had thus declared himself "King James's Man."

On entering Boston harbor they sailed across the bay, describing it as "very large" with "at least 50 islands in it." Once again the Pilgrims came face to face with the horrible ravages of the 1616 and 1617 plague. "Many, yea most of the islands had been inhabited; some being cleared from end to end. But the people are all dead or removed."

The few Indians they did meet "used us very kindly," the Pilgrims said, and shared their boiled cod. A chief told how his people had to keep on the move because they feared the Tarentines, a Maine tribe who raided them at harvest time to loot their crops. There the Pilgrims engaged in impromptu trading, forming an unusual scene near the shallop.

The Indian women "sold their coats from their backs and tied boughs about them, but with great shamefacedness, for indeed they are more modest than some of our English women are. We promised them to come again to them, and they us to keep their skins."

Because victuals were limited, Captain Standish and his men did not explore the Charles River, but did go several miles up the present Mystic River. Everywhere they were impressed, particularly by the great harbor. "Better harbors for shipping cannot be than here are," they judged. Indeed, in their report Bradford said that they came back to Plymouth "wishing they [their plantation] had been seated" by the future Boston Harbor.

In less than a decade new settlers—Puritans sharing the Pilgrims' New World dream—would sail into this same harbor and establish a community that, before the 1600s closed, would become the capital of the first permanent New England colony, the one the Pilgrims were striving to create at Plymouth.

By mid-September, harvest time had come to Plymouth. It was a "small harvest," said Bradford, but would provide a peck of corn a week per person. Winslow gave more detail. Squanto had advised them that spring in setting twenty acres of Indian corn. Besides, they had sowed six acres of barley and peas, "and according to the manner of the Indians, we manured our ground with herrings, or rather shads, which we have in great abundance, and take with great ease at our doors. . . .

"God be praised, we had a good increase of Indian corn, and our barley indifferent good, but our peas not worth the gathering, for we fear they were too late sown."

Winslow proceeded to write a brief, but still our most detailed description of the Pilgrims' first Thanksgiving. It was a harvest festival, probably some time in October. Neither Winslow nor Bradford agave an exact date. Bradford did tell gratefully how the Pilgrims had recovered their strength, and now had houses and food. Winslow, in his December 1621 letter to Morton, wrote:

"Our harvest being gotten in, our governor sent four men on fowling, that so we might, after a special manner, rejoice together after we had gathered the fruit of our labors. They four in one day killed as much fowl as, with a little help beside, served the company almost a week.

"At which time, amongst other recreations, we exercised our arms, many of the Indians coming amongst us, and among the rest, their greatest king, Massasoit, with some 90 men, whom for three days we entertained and feasted; and they went out and killed five deer, which they brought to the plantation, and bestowed on our governor, and upon the captain and others. And although it be not always so plentiful as it was at this time with us, yet by the goodness of God we are so far from want that we often wish you partakers of our plenty.

"We have found the Indians very faithful in their covenant of peace with us, very loving and ready to pleasure us. We often go to them and they come to us."

At last, after recurring hardship and suffering, the Pilgrims seemed to have found peace and plenty. In these weeks of exuberance Winslow declared: "If we have once but kine, horses and sheep, I make no question but men might live as contended here as in any part of the world." Winslow, in fact, would bring the first few cattle to Plymouth—still, that would not be for many more and difficult months.

The Pilgrims have left not the slightest uncertainty that their haven, for which they had patiently endured countless reverses, was primarily a religious community according to their interpretation of the Bible.

Thus Christmas Day 1621 was to them as any other day. Bradford dutifully called the Pilgrims to their work. But most of the London Strangers excused themselves. Bradford, after the manner of the tolerant Dutch, told them that "if they made it matter of conscience, he would spare them till they were better informed, so he led away the rest and left them." But when Bradford came home with the workers at noon:

"He found them [the London group] in the street at play, openly; some pitching the bar, and some at stool-ball [early cricket] and such like sports. So he went to them and took away their implements, and told them that it was against his conscience, that they should play and others work. If they made the keeping of it [Christmas] matter of devotion, let them keep their houses; but there should be no gaming or reveling in the streets. Since which time nothing hath been attempted that way, at least openly."

The Pilgrims celebrate their first harvest in Thanksgiving Feast, *by N. C. Wyeth.*

Newcomers Mean Short Rations

T he delight of that first Thanksgiving, and the high hopes that they would henceforth have an abundant larder and be blessed with assured peace, quickly faded.

For the Pilgrims, freedom from hunger would not be gained until after the unexpected heavy rain that miraculously saved the 1623 harvest. And the comforting proof that Massasoit was completely sincere would not come until that same year when an alert from Massasoit, conveyed by Hobomok, would help to preserve the colony's very life.

Celebration of the first Thanksgiving was hardly over when the Pilgrims, at first alarmed and then overjoyed, sighted the sails of the fifty-five-ton ship *Fortune* as it entered their harbor November 11, 1621. It was the first ship from overseas since the *Mayflower* departed. Aboard were thirty-five passengers, including "some wives and children" and future Governor Thomas Prence from Leyden, but mostly Strangers from the London area.

The newcomers also brought a problem, for they had exhausted their victuals; and when the *Fortune* left December 13, Bradford, after providing the crew food for their homeward voyage, felt forced to put the colony on "half allowance" (half rations)—a sudden reversal from the Pilgrims' festive Thanksgiving Day.

The *Fortune* had not been long gone when a messenger from the belligerent Narragansetts appeared at the plantation carrying a mysterious "bundle of new arrows lapped [wrapped] in a rattlesnake's skin."

Squanto explained that this was a challenge from the Narragansett sachem Canonicus. Bradford, always prompt to act in time of crisis, consulted the colony's leaders. Then, said Winslow, "the Governor stuffed the skin with powder and shot, and sent it back, returning no less defiance to

Canonicus," who probably was angry over his enemy Massasoit's links with the Pilgrims.

Dread of musket fire had spread to even the Narragansetts. When the rattlesnake skin arrived in the Indian camp, said Winslow, "it was no small terror to this savage king; insomuch as he would not once touch the powder or shot, or suffer it to stay in his house or country . . . and having been posted [sent] from place to place a long time, at length came back whole again."

To increase their security, the Pilgrims enclosed "their dwellings with a good strong pale, and made flankers in convenient places with gates to shut,

Going to Church, by N. C. Wyeth, depicts Pilgrims on their way to the meetinghouse on Burial Hill, which also served as a fort.

which were every night locked, and a watch kept." Captain Standish divided his men into four squadrons and assigned the places to which "they were to repair upon any sudden alarm."

This eight-foot-high palisade was completed by March. But the Pilgrims felt even stronger measures necessary when in June the shocking news came to them, from a passing fishing vessel, that three months earlier, on March 22, 1622, the Indians in Virginia had massacred 347 Jamestown settlers. This "deadly stroke" would contribute two years later to bankruptcy for the Virginia Company of London that had created the first permanent English colony in America.

On receiving the dreadful tidings the Pilgrims, despite their "weakness and time of wants," started that summer on a ten-month effort to build, on top of Burial Hill, "a fort with good timber, both strong and comely, which was of good defense, made with a flat roof and battlements, on which their ordnance were mounted, and where they kept constant watch." The structure, said Bradford, also served the Pilgrims "for a meeting house and was fitted accordingly for that use." Here the revered Elder Brewster, the colony's religious leader, "taught twice every Sabbath" for many years.

Danger to the colony's existence did not come, however, at this timber-fortress meeting house. Danger had been foreshadowed, though, in the previous November in a letter the *Fortune* brought from the adventurer Thomas Weston, that enterprising man, now grown callous and deceitful. The letter, said Bradford, was "full of complaints and expostulations." Weston rebuked the Pilgrims for, as he falsely imagined, wasting their time "in discoursing, arguing and consulting" because the *Mayflower* had returned with no cargo. He warned the Pilgrims that absence of profit would terminate support from the adventurers.

Weston's heartless letter was addressed to Governor Carver, whose dedication and toil had cost him his life. Bradford's response was prompt and pointed. He wrote Weston that great as were the costs to the adventurers, the loss of Carver's life "and many other honest and industrious men's lives cannot be valued at any price." He told of the Pilgrims' suffering so "that the living were scarce able to bury the dead." As for any who said that the Pilgrims were idle, "their hearts can tell their tongues they lie."

Weston, always protesting friendship, had written in his hard letter, "I promise you I will never quit the business." Yet the Pilgrims gathered in the following months that he had done just that, had quit "their joint stock," and was adventuring on his own.

In May 1622, seven men in a shallop came from Damariscove, off the Maine coast, where Weston had a large ship fishing. The men brought "no victuals nor any hope of any." Weston sent word that he was planning a colony and asked the Pilgrims meantime to house and to "entertain and supply" these men.

Weston did not stop there. Toward the end of June, he sent two ships with "some 50 or 60" more men to sponge on the Pilgrims, themselves hungry and confronted by famine. Some of these men were deserving, said Winslow, but most were a "stain on Old England that bred them." The Pilgrims fed them out of "compassion to the people . . . come into a wilderness," and in consideration of what Weston had "been unto them" and done for them in the past.

Still, the newcomers stole corn, made trouble, and repaid kindness with "secret backbitings and revilings." They even left their sick and lame behind in Plymouth when they took off at summer's end to establish Weston's colony at Wessagusset (Weymouth).

Instead of criticizing the Pilgrims, Weston would have served his ends better by following their example. Weston's men, by waste, disorder, and lack of leadership, gradually fell into such misery and dire straits—literally grubbing for food, some starving, some dying—as to bring upon them the contempt and enmity of their Indian neighbors they had wronged by stealing corn.

Leaders in the Massachusetts tribe began scheming with their Indian neighbors to rid themselves of Weston's colony. They quickly realized, however, said Winslow, that even if they spared the New Plymouth colony, the Pilgrims "would never leave the death of our countrymen unrevenged; and

therefore their safety could not be without the overthrow of both plantations."

One of the leading conspirators, husky, tall Wituwamat, was so confident of the result that, while seeking allies among the Cape Cod Indians, he declared in his native tongue, in the presence of the uncomprehending Captain Standish, that the English "died crying . . . more like children than men."

At this juncture, in March 1623, word reached Plymouth that Massasoit himself was sick and "like to die." Bradford at once sent Winslow "with some cordials to administer to him." Hobomok went as guide. Massasoit, blinded and suffering from days of constipation, was surrounded by his distressed followers, with the medicine man making "a hellish noise." Massasoit stretched out his hand to Winslow and said, "O Winslow, I shall never see thee again."

A cordial bottle had been accidentally broken en route, but Winslow gave the sachem "a confection of many comfortable conserves" and dissolved some of the confection in water for him to drink. Then, on sight returning, Winslow made the chief some duck broth. Massasoit's health, as if by magic, was restored after a few hours' sleep. Whereupon he declared, "I see the English are my friends . . . whilst I live I will never forget the kindness."

When Winslow was about to leave, Massasoit called Hobomok to the inner council of his warriors, "revealed the plot of the Massachusetts . . . and advised us to kill the men of the Massachusetts." Hobomok was told to tell this to Winslow, on the way home.

To thwart the plot, Bradford dispatched Captain Standish, along with eight picked colonists and Hobomok to go in the shallop to Wessagusset. There Standish helped the surviving Weston men quit their plantation after a fight that left seven Indians dead, among them Wituwamat.

The Pilgrims' speedy action "terrified and amazed" some of the absent conspirators, among them some of the nine chiefs who had signed the September 13, 1621 peace accord. These ran away "like men distracted, living in swamps and other desert [isolated] places," where some died. Others sent peace presents to Plymouth.

Massasoit, said Winslow, had saved the Pilgrims

"when we were at the pit's brim and . . . knew not that we were in danger." Any uncertainty about Massasoit's pledge of peace was now gone. Massasoit would live into his eighties to fall 1661, outliving all the early Pilgrim plantation leaders, and always he kept peace with the Pilgrims.

Nearly two years would pass before the plantation held its second Thanksgiving Day. At times famine would be almost as close as during the worst days at Wessagusset, with the Pilgrims, their corn supply low, "enforced to live on ground nuts, clams, muscles and such other things as naturally the country afforded." They even had to draw on their precious seed corn to furnish provisions for Standish during his rescue mission to Wessagusset.

The *Fortune's* arriving with "not so much as a biscuit cake or any other victuals," resulting both from the adventurers' penuriousness and the unusual four-month length of its passage, meant that the 1621 harvest so joyfully celebrated at first Thanksgiving had, almost overnight, become painfully inadequate.

Bradford's ordering "six months at half allowance" seemed inadequate by May 1622, when the Pilgrims' "provisions were wholly spent, and they looked hard for supply but none came." Winslow

Portrait of Edward Winslow was painted in London in 1651.

explained that even in a country where fish and fowl seem to abound, as during the first Thanksgiving, supply was controlled by the seasons. You just do not, he explained, "go into an orchard in the winter to gather cherries." As for fish, the Pilgrims at first lacked seines and proper tackle.

By the time that all of Weston's men arrived—the seven forerunners in May and the fifty to sixty in June—the Pilgrim colony found famine had begun "to pinch them sore." The arrival, also in June, of the fishermen's boat, though it brought the terrible news about the Jamestown massacre, was providential. Bradford sent Winslow in a Pilgrim boat, getting pilotage from the fishermen, to the Maine waters of Monhegan and Damariscove to get some provisions.

Several benefits came from this trip. The fishing captains in Maine, even to straining their own supplies, gladly contributed, and Winslow returned with "good quantity." The Pilgrims had also learned the route to Maine. Still, to make the supply hold until harvest, Bradford limited the distribution to "only a quarter pound of bread a day to each person . . . till corn was ripe."

The 1622 harvest was a poor one, chiefly because the Pilgrims could not tend the crop as they should have because "of their weakness for want of food." The harvest had also been reduced by Weston's men stealing green corn. As for purchasing corn, the Pilgrims faced a dilemma: "Markets there was none to go to but only the Indians" and the Pilgrims "had no trading commodities."

Providence again came to the rescue. The sixty-ton *Discovery*, on its way from Jamestown to England, came into Plymouth Harbor. Its captain, though he proved a greedy, unprincipled trader, did sell the Pilgrims a good supply of beads and knives that were "then good trade" with the Indians.

That fall and during winter 1623 the Pilgrims made several trips to barter for corn from the Indians.

In this period before the Pilgrims taught the Indians how to increase their corn crops by using the English hoe, the Indians did not plant corn to excess. Still the Pilgrims were able to acquire "about 26 to 28 hogsheads of corn and beans," which, said Bradford, "was more than the Indians could well spare in these parts." The season being "very tempestuous," some was cached with the Indians to be fetched in the springtime.

On one of the very first trips in September, while Bradford was trading in Cape Cod's present Pleasant Bay, Squanto was stricken with a fever and died within a few days. He was buried, deeply mourned, somewhere on the present Chatham-to-Orleans shore.

Planting time came in April 1623, when, with little corn supply left but "that preserved for seed . . . we thought best to leave off all other works and prosecute that as most necessary."

Bradford and the "chiefest amongst them" made a basic decision on hastening, if possible, the Pilgrims' freedom from famine. Despite the agreements made with the now-wavering adventurers, the Pilgrim leaders decided that the best way to get a better crop was to forego holding it in common and to let each be responsible for his own supply. As Bradford told it, "they should set corn every man for his own particular, and in that regard to trust to themselves; in all other things to go on in the general way as before."

And so, without its entailing any inheritance of the land, the Pilgrim leaders "assigned to every fami-ly a parcel of land according to the proportion of their number. "This," said Bradford, "had very good success, for it made all hands very industrious, so as much more corn was planted than otherwise would have been by any means the Governor or any other could use." Planting time extended through April and May.

None of this farming meant immediate supplies of food. Rations continued short. At times they would go to bed not "knowing where to have a bit of anything the next day." They did try fishing, but if the boat was away long or came back with little they "all went to seeking shellfish which, at low water, they digged out of the sand."

Two ships from London brought ninety-three more men, women, and children to the colony—the 240-ton *Anne* in mid-July 1623, and two weeks later the accompanying (for a while) *Little James*, a 44-ton pinnace.

These passengers on arriving in their Promised Land, and seeing the Pilgrims' "low and poor condition ashore . . . were much daunted and dismayed, and according to their divers humors were diversely

The March of Myles Standish *shows an Indian guide leading militia on patrol (lithograph after a painting by J. E. Baker).*

affected. Some wished themselves in England again, others fell aweeping, fancying their own misery in what they saw now in others, others pitying the distress they saw their friends had been long in, and still were under. In a word, all were full of sadness.

"And truly it was no marvel they should be thus affected, for they (the Pilgrims) were in a very low condition; many were ragged in apparel and some little better than half naked. But for food they were all alike, save some that had got a few peas of the ship that was last here."

The colony had been suffering a "great drought" from mid-May to mid-July so that the cornstalks that had been first set "began to send forth the ear before it came to half growth and that which was later not like to yield any at all." And the beans were "parched away as though they had been scorched before the fire. Now were our hopes overthrown and we discouraged. . . ."

The devout Pilgrims, "in this great distress," gathered in the new meeting house for a day of humiliation "more solemnly to humble ourselves together before the Lord by fasting and prayer."

"But, O, the mercy of our God!" exclaimed Winslow. "For though in the morning, when we assembled together, the heavens were as clear, and the drought as like to continue as ever it was, yet (our exercise continuing some eight or nine hours), before our departure, the weather was overcast, the clouds gathered together on all sides, and on the next morning distilled such soft, sweet, and moderate showers of rain, continuing some 14 days . . . as it was hard to say whether our withered corn, or drooping affections, were most quickened and revived; such was the bounty and goodness of our God.

"Of this the Indians, by means of Hobomok, took notice," said Winslow; and the transformation, added Bradford, "made the Indians astonished to behold." Neither writer gave the precise date for the second Thanksgiving Day they then held in Plymouth. It was in late July or early August. But of the celebration, Bradford rapturously observed:

"Instead of famine, now God gave them plenty, and the face of things was changed, to the rejoicing of the hearts of many. . . ."

"Any general want or famine hath not been amongst them since to this day."

Among the passengers who had arrived on the *Anne* was one who brought joy to the face of Governor Bradford. She was thirty-three-year-old Alice Carpenter Southworth, a widow about a year his junior, member of the Leyden congregation, living in London. She had come with her sister Juliana's family, Mr. and Mrs. George Morton and their four children.

Not many days passed after the ship's arrival before Alice, on August 14, 1623 became Bradford's bride.

Our only description of the wedding, and that brief, comes from a twenty-five-year-old member of the gentry, Emmanuel Altham, one of the colony's adventurers who had just recently arrived in Plymouth as military captain and supercargo of the *Little James*, intending to use the pinnace for trading and fishing for the colony. In a letter to his brother, Sir Edward, young Captain Altham told first about Massasoit's arrival for the wedding.

The sachem, "as proper a man as was ever seen in this country," said Altham, came with his squaw-sachem, the queen. Massasoit was attired "like the rest of his men, all naked but only a black wolf skin he wears upon his shoulder, and about the breadth of a span he wears beads about his middle.

"With him came four other kings and about six score men with their bows and arrows—where, when they came to our town, we saluted them with the shooting off of many muskets and training our men. And so all the bows and arrows was brought into the Governor's house, and he brought the governor three or four bucks and a turkey. And so we had very good pastime in seeing them [the Indians] dance, which is in such manner, with such noise that you would wonder.

"And now to say somewhat of the great cheer we had at the Governor's marriage. We had about 12 pasty [meat pie] venisons, besides others, pieces of roasted venison and other such good cheer in such quantity that I could wish you some of our share. For here we have the best grapes that ever you saw—and the biggest, and divers sorts of plums and nuts. . . ."

Any threat of famine—indeed, to their survival—seemed gone at last from Plymouth.

Overcoming
the Burden of Debt

Liberation from an onerous burden of debt was not so quickly achieved by the Pilgrims as reaping a satisfactory crop of corn or establishing peace with their neighbors.

For as hospitable as Holland had been, their twelve years of hard work in that country left them with funds far inadequate to finance a plantation in a distant new land. Debt did not alarm the Pilgrims, for they were conscientious, steady workmen and their modest manner of life was thoroughly thrifty. They always felt certain that in time they would be able to pay any debts, and that most willingly.

Still, few of them would have judged that repayment would take a full quarter of a century, and that even then, some of the leaders would have to turn over their own houses and land to satisfy the last of the creditors.

Fishing was at first believed a speedy way to rid the Pilgrims of debt. King James had a shrewd question back in 1618, when the Pilgrims' friends were seeking royal approval for the colony. The king had wondered what sort of profit there could be in Northern Virginia and had seemed quite satisfied that fishing would provide livelihoods.

The Pilgrims, whose early acquaintance with the sea was limited, were quite convinced that fishing would be the answer. Even in fall 1623, when Winslow sent his *Good News from New England* to be printed in London, he was still enthusiastic about fishing.

Fish in New England, he wrote, "was in as great abundance as in any other part of the world." He added persuasive argument: If English merchants could enrich themselves sending salt, men, and ships "at a great charge" (cost) to fish in New England, what may the planters (Pilgrims) "expect when once they are seated, and make most of their salt there, and employ themselves at least eight months fishing?"

After another year's experience, though, the Plymouth leaders' attitude was profoundly different. Even Captain Altham, at first confident that easy profit was to be made from the abundance the New World had to offer, became more realistic about the difficulty in converting abundance into profit after taking the *Little James* to Narragansett Bay and returning with only a small store of skins "to my exceeding great grief."

As for the Pilgrims and fishing, Altham went on to say that he found they had lacked proper equipment, which was an initial handicap, but that they also had an even more serious problem. "How is it possible," asked Altham, "that those men that never saw fishing in their lives should raise profit by fishing?" A Plymouth colony investor himself, Altham warned in his 1624 letter to his brother, "This I say to you, that unless some other means be taken . . . no means of profit can be raised to the adventurers for their money again."

In that same year, Bradford gave his ultimate judgment on what fishing had done for the plantation, an opinion prompted by the fact that the 100-ton *Charity* was about to leave Plymouth to fish off Cape Ann. The ship, as the adventurers desired, was to establish a fish-curing stage (light wharf) on Cape Ann under a new patent. "Fishing," declared disillusioned Bradford, "—a thing fatal to this plantation."

Bradford had reasons aplenty for his pessimism. The *Charity*, whose departure from London had been delayed by disputes among the adventurers, turned out to be "too late for the fishing season." Besides, said Bradford, the ship's master was "a very drunken beast"; the man sent from London to make salt was an incompetent; and the ship's carpenter, sent to build boats, a good man, died of a fever after building but two shallops.

Moreover, the *Little James*, after being forced by a

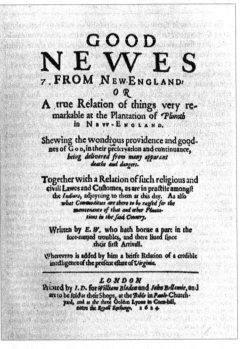

GOOD
NEWES
7. FROM NEW-ENGLAND:
OR
A true Relation of things very remarkable at the Plantation of *Plimoth* in NEW-ENGLAND.

Shewing the wondrous providence and goodnes of GOD, in their preservation and continuance, *being delivered from many apparant deaths and dangers.*

Together with a Relation of such religious and civill Lawes and Customes, as are in practise amongst the *Indians*, adjoyning to them at this day. As also what Commodities are there to be raysed for the maintenance of that and other Plantations in the said Country.

Written by E. W. who hath borne a part in the fore-named troubles, and there lived since their first Arrivall.

Whereunto is added by him a briefe Relation of a credible intelligence of the present estate of *Virginia.*

LONDON
Printed by I. D. for *William Bladen* and *John Bellamie*, and are to be sold at their Shops, at the *Bible* in *Pauls-Church-yard*, and at the three Golden Lyons in *Corn-hill*, neere the *Royall Exchange*. 1624

Edward Winslow's optimistic account of early Plymouth was published in 1624 (title page is shown).

storm in Narragansett Bay to "cut our mainmast overboard," was driven by another storm upon rocks at Damariscove, and then sank with the master and two sailors lost. The ship was later salvaged, but all these heavy costs were added to the Pilgrims' debt.

The *Charity*, on its March 1624 arrival in Plymouth, had nevertheless brought something that would provide a tremendous benefit to the plantation. Winslow, returning from a diplomatic mission in England, had fetched with him "the first beginning of any cattle" in New England—three heifers and a bull. Their recognition as a godsend to Plymouth's prosperity would not occur for several years or until livestock later became one of the two main sources for discharging the Pilgrims' ever-mounting debt.

The other was fur, especially beaver, which would lead to exploration, expansion, and establishment of trade. This development too was slow because the Pilgrims on arrival were "altogether unprovided for trade." Neither, Bradford continued, "was there any amongst them that ever saw a beaver skin till they came here and were informed by Squanto."

The Pilgrims had brought "a few trifling commodities" and later acquired some beads and knives that helped in earliest meetings with the Indians. Samoset and Squanto had brought "some few skins to truck" on that wonderful day when Massasoit first appeared on Watson's Hill and Captain Standish and Winslow, on their first visit to the future Boston Bay, had obtained a "considerable quantity of beaver" from the modest Indian squaws. Those were the Pilgrim beginnings of trade in fur.

By the time Bradford gave his baleful appraisal of fishing, the Pilgrims had learned how to bring in plentiful harvests.

Corn, completely home-grown, was superb for

barter. "They began now highly to prize corn as more precious than silver," said Bradford, "for money they had none, and if any had, corn was preferred before it." The 1625 harvest was abundant, and the year so pleasant that Bradford declared that the Pilgrims had "never felt the sweetness of the country till this year."

The Pilgrims then tried something new: freighting corn in one of the shallops that the *Charity's* carpenter had built after they had "laid a little deck over her midships to keep the corn dry." Having no seamen, Bradford sent the dauntless Winslow and some other old planters eastward to Maine—the route Winslow had sailed to seek food from the fishing fleet during 1622, the year of near starvation. This time he went to seek trade.

Few episodes in our early history are more courageous or daring than Winslow's sailing beyond Damariscove and Monhegan to the Kennebec River and miles up this strange river to the present site of Augusta, the capital of Maine, then an Indian village called Cushnoc. "God preserved them," said Bradford, and the enterprise "brought home 700 pounds of beaver . . . having little or nothing else but this corn which themselves had raised out of the earth." The Pilgrims had thus arrived at the threshold of extensive "trucking."

Meantime, particularly in the years 1624 to 1626, the financial arrangements between the Pilgrims and the adventurers were changing drastically. Purse strings in London, far from liberal from the start, tightened when the *Mayflower* returned without profit.

To keep open the Pilgrims' only source of credit, Robert Cushman had come over on the *Fortune* in November 1621, to get the Pilgrims to sign the harsh terms of their business agreement that the Pilgrims had rejected when the *Mayflower* was about to weigh anchor at Southampton. This time, said Bradford, the Pilgrims "yielded . . . to Cushman's persuasion." That the Pilgrims had loaded the *Fortune* with "good clapboard as full as she could stow and two hogsheads of beaver and otter skins" loosened the adventurers' purse strings, even though the cargo was pillaged by French pirates who seized, then released, the plundered *Fortune* on its way back.

Weston's withdrawal from the joint stock company was followed by others as voyages by the *Anne*, the *Little James* (which was later captured along with its crew by Barbary pirates operating in the English Channel), and the *Charity* failed to produce anticipated profits. Two years of cross-ocean negotiations conducted by Isaac Allerton for the colony produced a new business agreement, signed November 16, 1626.

Only forty-two of the original seventy-odd adventurers signed in London. Some had withdrawn for reasons other than lacking profit. Official persecution of religious dissent had been increasing in England under the second Stuart king, Charles I. Adventurers responsive to the throne, and sensitive about the Pilgrims' separatism, had blocked the Pilgrims' beloved pastor, Rev. John Robinson, and others in the Leyden congregation, from emigrating to Plymouth.

Under the new business agreement Governor Bradford and seven other Pilgrim leaders, calling themselves the "undertakers," agreed to pay off 1,800 English pounds at 200 pounds each year at the Royal Exchange in London, besides "some 600 more" pounds in other debt. This commitment made possible a 1627 division of land in Plymouth, among the 156 colonists, with each group of six receiving a cow,

Aptucxet Trading Post was rebuilt on the original 1627 Pilgrim foundation near Cape Cod Canal in Bourne.

two goats, and some swine. The undertakers were granted full control—a monopoly—of the colony's trade for six years to help discharge the debt "which lay so heavily" on the colony.

To make trading easier the Pilgrims in 1627 built a small pinnace at Manomet, then on Buzzards Bay, "a place 20 miles from the plantation." Bradford had first seen Manomet in January 1623, when seeking corn for the nearly starving colonists at Plymouth. He went roughly along the route of the present Cape Cod Canal, up Scusset Creek on the east to the short carrying place and then down the small Manomet River to Buzzard's Bay on the west.

The Pilgrims built, near the bay in Manomet, a "house of hewn oak planks, called Aptucxet, where they keep two men, winter and summer, in order to maintain trade and possession."

Those words are in an eyewitness account from the secretary of New Amsterdam (Manhattan), Isaak de Rasieres, who in October 1627, after an exchange of letters with Bradford, came via Aptucxet to Plymouth to discuss trade.

The Dutch had converted trading posts into settlements at Albany in 1624 and New Amsterdam in 1626. De Rasieres on this visit introduced the Pilgrims to wampum—shell beads used as money by the Indians—in the hope, he said, of getting the Pilgrims to trade for wampum and thus keeping the Pilgrims from discovering fur trade with Indians living to the westward.

But, pressed by debt, the Pilgrims went ahead anyway. Some Indians who had been driven from the Connecticut River Valley by rival Indians, the Pequots, urged the Pilgrims to trade for furs. In summer 1632, fearless Edward Winslow became the first Englishman to sail up the Connecticut River for discovery and trade. Winslow even selected the site where the Pilgrims would a year later found Windsor, one of Connecticut's oldest settlements.

In 1633 Winslow was elected governor, temporarily replacing Bradford. In September of that year Governor Winslow sent a different leader, Lieutenant William Holmes, to Connecticut.

To get ahead of these English, the Dutch had three months earlier established a "slight fort and planted two pieces of ordnance" at the present Hartford. But despite Dutch threats to fire on them, Lieutenant Holmes and his Pilgrim companions sailed a short way upriver to the Windsor site they had bought from the Indians. On September 26, they "clapped up" the small frame house they had brought in their bark and surrounded it with a palisade. Here they traded for furs until 1637. By then they had sold off most of their land to the more numerous emi-

Lieutenant Holmes and Pilgrims sailed up the Connecticut River in 1633 and erected the first house in present Windsor, Connecticut.

grants coming westward from the Puritan colony John Winthrop had founded in 1630 at Boston.

On the Penobscot River in Maine, the Pilgrims' debt grew heavier when French colonists from Acadia in eastern, coastal Canada, in 1631 robbed and in 1635 took over the Pilgrim trading post near the present Castine, a venture in which the Pilgrims had been reluctantly involved by their agent Isaac Allerton. On the Kennebec River, however, profit from the fur trade contributed heavily to clearing the Pilgrims of debt.

After Winslow's discovery of the Indian village below the Kennebec falls, Allerton in 1628 secured a patent in London so that the Pilgrims could have a solid claim in the area.

The Pilgrims erected a house on the site of the present Fort Western, which is diagonally across the river from Maine's present state capital. They stocked it with corn and commodities that fishermen had traded to them: "coats, shirts, rugs and blankets, biscuits, peas, prunes, etc."

The Dutch had been right about wampum. The Pilgrims could scarce obtain enough for the eager inland Indians.

Allerton's 1628 patent, however, proved to be so "ill-bounded," leaving the Cushnoc area open to rivals, that the Pilgrims sought a renewal. On January 13, 1630 the Warwick Patent, though it pertained chiefly to the Plymouth Colony, also clearly defined the Kennebec grant. This precision probably was attributable to Winslow's extensive knowledge of the Indians and the wilderness. The patent covered miles along the Kennebec River at the present Augusta, and fifteen miles inland on either side of the river.

Tons of beaver and other furs were freighted for years from here to the British market through the Pilgrims' partners in London.

After the new business arrangement was signed in November 1626, four of the London adventurers functioned as factors for the Pilgrims, receiving, storing, and selling shipments, and purchasing requested commodities. These Londoners also acted as partners and provided credit.

As Pilgrim trade expanded, so too did the record of transactions. The Pilgrims, not highly experienced as businessmen, were completely trusting. Cross-

Atlantic differences arose as the record grew increasingly lengthy and confusing.

A profoundly embarrassing development was the Pilgrims' coming to belive that Isaac Allerton, long their agent in dealing with the adventurers abroad, had, Bradford said, "played his own game" and led the Pilgrims "into the briars." They felt that losses and expenses he had incurred on his own had been charged to them. Winslow was chosen to replace Allerton as agent. Allerton left the plantation, tried business ventures, fishing, and trading, and died in New Haven.

The disputed sums exceeded by many times the 1,800 English pounds mentioned in the 1626 agreement. Plymouth and London disagreed fundamentally on the size of the debt. Despite the quantities of records extant, a positive judgment is elusive. The records were sloppy, some items being charged three times. Fluctuations in prices and usurious interest rates—as high as 50 percent—produced misunderstandings, sharp letters, and even had the London adventurers suing one another.

The leaders in Plymouth, though they felt they had "to sustain [bear] the greatest wrong," were growing aged and "were loath to leave these entanglements upon their children." So in a "composition by mutual agreement" on October 15, 1641, the parties on both sides of the ocean fixed the amount of the debt. And when the Londoners signed it, in 1642, they benevolently agreed that the Londoners' proceeds were to be used for church purposes in both the new Bay Colony and the Plymouth Colony.

One of the Londoners did hold out, still demanding payment on a separate disputed debt. Finally, in 1645, Bradford and his fellow undertakers, to terminate all claims, agreed to pay this demand even though one of the claimant's fellow adventurers declared that no "good proof" for the claim existed. It was paid by Bradford, Winslow, Standish, and others, selling some of their houses and many acres of land, both in Plymouth and in the newer Pilgrim towns, Rehoboth and Marshfield.

At last, title to the haven for which the Pilgrims had for years been sacrificing and patiently laboring was completely theirs.

New Plymouth Joins the Bay Colony

Plymouth's position as the prime community and seaport in New England was drastically changed in just a few years by a rising tide of Puritan colonization that began in 1628.

On September 6, 1628, the 120-ton *Abigail*, which had left England about eleven weeks earlier, sailed past Cape Ann into the Naumkeag harbor. On board was the willful, austere John Endecott with some forty colonists, along with cattle and supplies, come to prepare the way for larger contingents of settlers in the then embryonic Massachusetts Bay Company.

At the time Endecott arrived the Naumkeag colony was being run by a sturdy Puritan, Roger Conant, who had arrived on his own in Plymouth on the *Anne* in 1623, had left in the following year, and had gone on to form Naumkeag in 1626.

Happily, Endecott and Conant's "old settlers" were able to compose their differences and promptly, in gratitude, the Naumkeag plantation was renamed Salem—a Biblical word for peace.

By winter 1628-1629, Salem was suffering difficulties such as the Pilgrims had experienced in their early years—privations and illness. Many, including Endecott's wife, were fatally stricken. Endecott appealed to Governor Bradford for help, and Bradford dispatched Plymouth's only physician, Samuel Fuller, after which Endecott thanked Bradford for his "kind love and care in sending Mr. Fuller amongst us." This intercolony friendship would be lasting.

Plymouth's population of roughly 200 was exceeded in 1629 when six vessels arrived in Salem with 406 settlers sent by the Massachusetts Bay Company. These vessels delivered to the Puritans an impressive copy of the new Massachusetts Bay charter that King Charles had approved March 4, 1629, along with provisions, cows, goats, horses, and "great pieces of ordnance."

The Pilgrims welcomed some new settlers for whom Plymouth had been waiting many years—forty-five of the Leyden congregation were among the passengers on two of the vessels that arrived in Salem. Their passage had been arranged through Isaac Allerton in London, and the cost was contentedly added to the Pilgrim debt. Among these Pilgrims was nineteen-year-old Thomas Willet, who would ably serve the Plymouth Colony and would one day become the first English mayor of New York City.

Fuller's influence on Salem's settlers was far more than medicinal. Fuller had been a deacon since 1609 in Leyden and in the zealous Endecott he found an admiring supporter. Endecott even wrote to Bradford, in May 1629, that Fuller had satisfied him "touching your judgments of the outward form of God's worship. It is, as far as I can gather, no other than is warranted by the evidence of truth."

Endecott lost no time in acting on this belief. On July 20, about a month after the 1629 ship arrivals began, Endecott held "a solemn day of humiliation" to select, in Plymouth's fashion, a pastor and a ministerial teacher. And he picked the following August 6 for another day of humiliation, to choose elders and deacons.

Headwinds prevented Governor Bradford and other Plymouth leaders from reaching Salem in time for the ordinations, but they got there to join the feasting and to extend "the right hand of fellowship."

Thus the first Congregational Church, in the manner Fuller had described to Endecott, was organized in the Bay State. The covenant adopted by the settlers is still extant.

Among the clergy who had come over in the 1629 ships was a separatist Cambridge University graduate, Rev. Ralph Smith. Rev. Smith, after serving briefly as minister to a small struggling settlement at Nantasket (Hull) on outer Boston Harbor, late in that year was chosen and ordained the first pastor of the church in Plymouth in the same way as Salem had organized its church in the prior summer. The Pilgrims' faithful pastor, Rev. Robinson, had died in Leyden March 1, 1625.

Plymouth's ascendancy as New England's foremost port plainly declined in June and July 1630 when Governor John Winthrop arrived with the original Massachusetts Bay charter and eleven ships, 700 settlers, and tons of supplies—the largest fleet of colonists that had set sail from England.

Besides hundreds of sailors to man the ships, the overall number of settlers would approximate 1,000. In May, preceding Winthrop's eleven ships, two others in this emigration from the west of England brought 220 settlers who would organize the town of Dorchester. Four more ships would arrive later in the year, one of the last being the *Handmaid* from London, which, before proceeding to Boston, left forty-seven of its sixty passengers at Plymouth. These were the last of the Leyden congregation brought over by the Pilgrims.

"As one small candle may light a thousand," said Bradford, the light kindled by Plymouth "hath shone unto many, yea in some sort to our whole nation. Let the glorious name of Jehovah have all the praise."

Plymouth had long been seen as a beacon for other colonists. One of our earliest historians, Rev. William Hubbard, a friend of Roger Conant, the "old settler of Naumkeag," wrote that the fame of Plymouth, "with the success thereof, was spread abroad" and encouraged investors. Nine of the adventurers who invested in the Plymouth plantation, particularly London merchant Robert Keayne, who would come to Boston in 1635 and found the Ancient and Honorable Artillery Company, also became leading investors in the Massachusetts Bay Company. Another of those investors wrote to Governor Bradford in 1632: "Had not you and we joined and continued together, New England might yet have been scarce known."

Friendship continued to grow between Plymouth and Boston settlers, for they were more naturally companions than rivals. Religious convictions had inspired both to migrate, and their religious difference was mostly in their degree of Puritanism.

Deacon Fuller, who kept up his ministrations to the newcomers' sick and dying, wrote to Bradford about a Puritan leader who told him that Rev. John Cotton, as Winthrop's ships were about to leave Southampton, had instructed his former parishioners: "They should take advice of them at Plymouth and should do nothing to offend them."

Winthrop and Bradford made visits to each

other's colonies. They also consulted on problems. An immediate, grievous difficulty for Plymouth, a highly law-abiding community, was how it should deal with its first murder, which occurred just a few weeks after Winthrop's arrival. This crime came in the very month (September 1630) when the Puritans rechristened "Trimountaine," naming it Boston in honor of Rev. John Cotton, who had come from Boston in Lincolnshire.

Governor John Winthrop, first leader of the Bay colony

Violent and profane John Billington of London had waylaid a young man in Plymouth, after a quarrel, and shot him. Winthrop, said Bradford, "concurred with them that he ought to die and the land be purged from blood." Billington had been "found guilty of willful murder by plain and notorious evidence . . . and was for the same accordingly executed." It was the first of the very few executions in Plymouth.

Compared to neighboring Plymouth colony, the Bay's growth in population was meteoric. Fully 200 ships, with emigrants fleeing the dictatorial, disintegrating rule of King Charles I, arrived in Boston during the 1630s. By 1635, the colony's population was 7,000 (which Plymouth would not approach until the late 1670s), and by 1640 the Bay had 16,000 settlers.

Their arrival in the Bay, with many moving into the interior, created a highly profitable market, of which Bradford wrote: "It pleased God in these times so to bless the country with such access and confluence of people into it, as it was thereby much enriched, and cattle of all kinds stood at a high rate for divers years together. . . . Corn also went at a round rate." And so did the English wheat they had started planting in the Plymouth colony.

Boston, with its far broader and deeper harbor than Plymouth's, had quickly become the New England center for trade, commerce, and finance. Plymouth, exchanging its cattle, corn, and wheat, could more advantageously obtain its English necessities in the Boston market rather than in London.

When the London adventurers came to settling accounts with Plymouth, one of the transactions was completed by Governor Bradford's sending cattle to Boston to settle an adventurer's account with Governor Winthrop.

The Rev. Roger Williams, who was banished from the Bay Colony in 1636, had been in New England five years and had resided in both Plymouth and Boston. When with Governor Winthrop's covert help, the Rev. Williams fled to escape deportation to England, he was certainly a first-hand and unprejudiced observer as he described Boston—only five years after its founding—as "The chief mart and port of New England."

Governor Bradford, with church in mind rather than seeking "the enriching of themselves," was always eager to keep the original Pilgrim congregation intact in Plymouth. But the need for more land for farms and pasturage for cattle powerfully attracted Pilgrims to more plentiful and arable nearby land, at first in Kingston on the Jones River, Duxbury on Plymouth Bay, and Marshfield.

The profitable Boston market also multiplied Plymouth communities as children of the early Pilgrims sought to own their own farms. Some Puritan newcomers chose to create homesteads within the Plymouth colony, particularly in its western region, and these looked more to Boston than to Plymouth as their market and commercial center.

On March 2, 1641, when Governor Bradford assigned to the growing body of freemen the 1630 Warwick patent that had granted Plymouth colony to him, Bradford listed the "divers townships" as these ten: Plymouth, Duxbury, Scituate, Taunton, Sandwich, Yarmouth, Barnstable, Marshfield, Seekonk (later called Rehoboth), and Nauset (later called Eastham).

By 1640 the famed Long Parliament had assembled in England, a prelude to Great Britain's civil war, which brought King Charles to the chopping block and elevated Oliver Cromwell to be Lord Protector of the Puritan Commonwealth. The gathering civil storm brought the great emigration to New England to a halt—in fact, many Bay Puritans headed back to England to take part in the struggle.

The price of cattle, corn, and wheat in the Boston market plummeted. Yet the self-reliant Plymouth settlers, almost all involved in farming, were able to manage. And gradually, the depression was much relieved as trade, via Boston, opened with the West Indies.

The exodus from Plymouth for better and more land had led Bradford and those remaining to consider moving in 1644 as a church body to Nauset on Cape Cod. A group, sent there to study the suggestion, advised that they would be wiser to remain in Plymouth with its better harbor and sufficient space for the entire remaining congregation. Some went anyway to Nauset, leading Bradford, who was seeking to hold the church body together, to grieve:

"Thus was this poor church left, like an ancient mother grown old and forsaken of her children . . . and she like a widow left only to trust in God."

On the death of Elder Brewster April 18, 1643, Bradford, an orphan who had been like a son to Brewster, marveled at the Pilgrim fathers' longevity despite "what crosses, troubles, fears, wants, and sorrows they had been liable unto. . . . What was it that upheld them? It was God's visitation that preserved their spirits."

Brewster was "near 80" when he died. Edward Winslow, Bradford's sturdy lieutenant and thrice chosen to serve as governor, went to England on several missions as the colony's agent and died at sea in the West Indies on military service for Oliver Cromwell in 1655. Winslow was nearly sixty. Valiant Captain Myles Standish died in his house at the foot of Captain's Hill in Duxbury, October 3, 1656. He was seventy-two.

Bradford himself, who had been elected thirty times as the Pilgrim governor, died May 8, 1657 at sixty-seven. His death was, Rev. Cotton Mather said, "lamented by all the colonies of New England," for he was regarded "as a common blessing and father to them all." Bradford had devoted much of his final year to study of still another tongue, Hebrew, "to see with my own eyes something of that most ancient

language, and holy tongue . . . in which God and the angels spoke to the holy patriarchs of old time."

Bradford died in his dwelling on the main street of Plymouth, at the northwest corner where New England's oldest street, Leyden Street, crosses the main street—diagonally opposite the corner where Elder Brewster had lived so many years. Bradford's remains were carried up Burial Hill, directly in back of his house and garden, and were interred. He was the last of the Pilgrim Fathers—and in the neighboring Bay colony even Governor John Winthrop, his friend, had predeceased him.

Protecting the settlers' security, their defense, had been a problem from the moment the Pilgrims arrived and began exploring Cape Cod. Defense continued a vital need throughout the plantation's life, and ultimately became the decisive factor in the royal action in London that would bring to a close independent governance for the Plymouth Colony.

Fearless Captain Standish, with his militia band, was long the Pilgrims' shield, and the peace with Massasoit was long their guarantee. Plymouth over the years stood ready to help in each of the New England region's wars. In 1637, after an appeal from Governor Winthrop, Plymouth had a bark and fifty armed men ready to shove off for the Pequot War in Connecticut when word came from the Bay that "the enemy was as good as vanquished."

In 1643, Bradford reported that Massasoit's enemies, the Narragansetts, had been plotting against the English "ever since the Pequot War." In that year Plymouth, with the colonies of Massachusetts Bay, Connecticut (then the area around Hartford), and New Haven combined in a New England Confederation to protect themselves from the Narragansetts. They also wanted to be prepared against raids by the French or Dutch now that England's civil war had erupted in 1642 and was then raging.

In the calamitous 1675 to 1676 war with King Philip, son of Massasoit, the Plymouth Colony, though least populous and prosperous among the New England Confederation colonies, was a crucial participant.

Governor Josiah Winslow, eldest son of Governor Edward Winslow, served as commander-in-chief of the Confederation militia in the bloody Great Swamp

Fight, December 19, 1675, a battle that eliminated the powerful Narragansetts, then a key alley of King Philip, as a combat force.

It was also Governor Josiah Winslow who called Captain Benjamin Church from services in the Plymouth meeting house and sent him on the mission during which Church, along with friendly Indians, tracked down King Philip in a Mt. Hope swamp (in the present Bristol, R.I.) on August 12, 1676. This battle ended the warfare that had left hardly a colonial family without a war victim, thirteen of the Bay and Plymouth colonies' seventy-five towns destroyed, with forty others ravaged by flames.

Following the Glorious Revolution of 1688 that deposed King James II, last of the Stuart kings, Plymouth once again tried, like the rest of the New England colonies, to obtain charter.

Charters of all the New England colonies had been vacated and King James II had set up Sir Edmund Andros as governor of the Dominion of New England. Andros had ruled with his royally picked council and with all the colonists' hard-won self-government abolished. When news of the Glorious Revolution reached Boston in April 1689, Andros, amid great rejoicing, was promptly imprisoned there and held for shipment to England.

Plymouth, unlike its neighboring colonies, had never had a charter. At the time it had received the Warwick patent, back in 1630, Plymouth had tried hard to get a charter. Two of the London adventurers did write to Governor Bradford that King James I had "graciously" assented to Plymouth's request, but somehow the charter got lost in the Lord Keeper's and the Solicitor's bureaucracies. The adventurers explained: "Many locks must be opened with the silver, nay the golden key." This category, of course, excluded the Pilgrims, who had piles of debts, not of silver and gold.

Prospects for obtaining a charter again seemed excellent after Governor Josiah Winslow's successes in King Philip's War. King Charles II was agreeable, and even wrote to Governor Winslow promising a charter. But Winslow, only fifty-two, was stricken by a fatal illness as he was completing arrangements with London to get the charter. And by the time Plymouth tried again, the court's attitude had

changed and charters, like the Bay's, were being revoked.

New warfare in the late 1600s dimmed Plymouth's final hopes for a charter. The Pilgrims were still suffering from the staggering loss in lives and property Plymouth sustained in King Philip's War when new demands came. By 1688 another conflict, King William's War, an eight-year struggle, was under way, the first in nearly a century of recurrent conflicts between French and English for domination of America.

Plymouth quickly encountered difficulties when it began pressing its towns for yet more men and more war taxes. It also found itself unable to raise sufficient funds to send to London to finance the quest for a charter, even though, for a two-year period, the Massachusetts, New York, Rhode Island, and Connecticut colonies were maneuvering to take over Plymouth in new charters they were seeking.

Finally, when on October 7, 1691 King William III had the great seal affixed to the new charter of the Massachusetts Bay, Plymouth colony was included in the New England territory of the Bay colony along with Martha's Vineyard and Nantucket Island—both of which had belonged to New York—and all of Maine.

King William and the Privy Council embedded in the wording of the 1691 Bay Charter the reason for including the Plymouth colony. It was included, the charter reads, so that "our colony of New Plymouth in New England may be brought under such a form of government as may put them in a better condition of defense."

Any doubt about this intent was certainly dispelled when the man who negotiated the Bay Charter, Rev. Increase Mather, returned to wartime Boston with the new royal governor, Sir William Phips, Reverend Mather's parishioner in Boston's then Old North Church in old North Square. Phips, first governor of the Bay and Plymouth, had already commanded military campaigns in Nova Scotia and Quebec. Besides being named royal governor, he was to be military commander-in-chief of all the New England colonies.

At the time some suspected that Reverend Mather's extensive influence in London had brought about the merger. But most in Plymouth, which would eventually organize a Day of Thanksgiving, soon seemed content.

Economically, agricultural Plymouth had long been a supplier to the Bay. The religions of the two colonies, the rock on which both had been founded, were just about the same. And the union with the most populous and wealthy of the New England colonies gave Plymouth immediate assurance of strong defense.

For most Pilgrims the transition was easy and natural. For Plymouth the biggest change was that citizens in Plymouth territory—the three counties into which the colony had been divided in 1685, roughly the present Plymouth, Bristol, and Barnstable Counties—looked henceforth to Boston as the colony's capital, and the elected deputies from the towns sat in the Great and General Court in Boston.

In 1620 when the Pilgrims embarked "to begin," as Edward Winslow called it, "the great work of plantation in New England," they had received a letter at Southampton from their pastor in Leyden, the Rev. John Robinson. The pastor commented that they were about to become "a body politic using amongst yourselves civil government." Their objective and that of their chosen magistrates should always be, he advised, to "Diligently promote the common good."

The colony's population near the close of the seventeenth century attained only 13,000 inhabitants. These included some Indians within their territory and some blacks. Records, though meager, show the colony's first black male on a militia availability list in 1643 and the first black woman in 1653. No names appeared.

Generally, the Pilgrims were, for their era, tolerant. They never hanged or burned religious dissenters. They had but two witch trials, one ending in a not-guilty verdict, the other in the accuser's being fined for slander. Overall, the Pilgrims were impressively law-abiding people. They did not even set up a jailhouse during the colony's first two decades.

In 1691, when the colony's future was being decided by the king and Privy Council in London, the economic consequences of King Philip's War along with King William's War, calling for ever-greater levies of men and money, were splitting the colony. Taxes were so onerous on some of the colony's seventeen towns that they simply were not met. Many towns, indeed, had not been able for years to support the local minister.

Some criticized the Plymouth colony's last governor, Thomas Hinckley, for not trying harder to secure a charter. Hinckley, though, had served the colony long and faithfully. He had fought in the crucial Great Swamp battle. Starting as a deputy from his Cape Cod town, Barnstable, he had gone on to serve as assistant to the governor, beginning in 1658, and in 1680, when he was sixty-two, he had become the colony's sixth governor.

Hinckley held that office, save for the autocratic year under Sir Edmund Andros, until the office itself was terminated.

Hinckley, beset by many difficulties during his final years in the governorship, left the impression that he had come to believe that his fellow citizens' future would be brighter and Pilgrim ideals would be better preserved by union with the more stable and prosperous Bay colony—that this union would truly, as expressed by Rev. Robinson, "promote the common good."

Just as the old colony had a Bradford to help lead at the beginning, another was instrumental in the transition.

Major William Bradford, Jr., son and namesake of the Pilgrim father, presided at the last Court of Assistants that met in Plymouth April 5, 1692. Major Bradford, deputy governor from 1682 to the end, had served the colony in many important posts. He commanded one of its two companies of militia in King Philip's War and suffered serious wounds in the Great Swamp battle.

Before Plymouth would hold its next election—scheduled for 1692—Royal Governor Phips arrived from England, and the new colonial government, now including the Bay's fifty-eight towns, was established in Boston. There the legislature met, and sitting in the upper branch were both Plymouth's former governor Hinckley and former deputy governor William Bradford, Jr.

All opportunities available to Bay Staters were now equally open to citizens in New England's oldest colony.

Like other Pilgrim descendants, the Bradfords over the years would fill many vital public functions in the Bay Colony, even that of chief executive of the future Commonwealth, a position to which another Bradford, Governor Robert F. Bradford, direct descendant of Gov. William Bradford, builder of the 1600s Plymouth colony, was elected by his fellow Bay Staters in mid-20th century.

Sir William Phips was the first governor of the combined Bay and Plymouth colonies and military commander of all New England colonies.

The Great Swamp Fight of December 19, 1675, in which King Phillip's powerful allies, the Narragansetts, were eliminated as a combat force.

ART CREDITS

Maps on pp. 2, 16, 40, 63 by Deborah Perugi, reprinted courtesy of *The Boston Globe;* pp. 3 top, 3 bottom, 5: copyright reserved to Her Majesty Queen Elizabeth II; pp. 4 top, 4 bottom, 6, 8 right, 12, 13, 16 bottom, 17, 20, 25 left, 25 right, 42, 44 left, 44 right, 45, 49 bottom, 51, 77, 83, 95: photographs by William Ryerson, reprinted courtesy of *The Boston Globe;* p. 8 left: reproduced by kind permission of the vicar and churchwardens, Parish of Boston, England; p. 10: reprinted by permission of the Borthwick Institute; p. 30: photograph by William Ryerson, reprinted courtesy of *The Boston Globe* (reproduced by permission of the First Parish Unitarian Universalist Church, Plymouth, Mass.); p. 14: photograph by William Ryerson, reprinted courtesy of *The Boston Globe* (reproduced by permission of All Saints' Church, Babworth); p. 17 left: photograph by William Ryerson, reprinted courtesy of *The Boston Globe* (reproduced courtesy of the Boston Borough Council, Boston, England); pp. 18, 26, 29 bottom, 33, 64, 67: reprinted by permission of the Boston Athenaeum; pp. 19, 22: from the Collection Gemeentearchief Amsterdam; p. 24: photograph by William Ryerson, reprinted courtesy of *The Boston Globe* (from the Pilgrim Collection, Gemeentearchief Leiden); pp. ii, viii, 28, 29 top, 41, 56, 59, 70, 73, 79, 90, 91: photographs by William Ryerson, reprinted courtesy of *The Boston Globe* (reproduced by permission of the Pilgrim Hall Museum, Plymouth, Mass.); p. 34: reprinted by permission of the Parish of St. Mary, Rotherhithe; p. 48: reprinted by permission of the City Art Gallery of Bristol, England; p. 49 top: source unknown; pp. 54, 101, 105 top: photographs by William Ryerson, reprinted courtesy of *The Boston Globe* (reproduced courtesy of the Commonwealth of Massachusetts Art Commission); pp. 60, 62: photographs by William Ryerson, reprinted courtesy of *The Boston Globe* (reproduced by permission of the Pilgrim Monument & Provincetown Museum); pp. 76, 80, 88: photographs by William Ryerson, reprinted courtesy of *The Boston Globe* (from the collection of the Metropolitan Life Insurance Company, NYC); pp. 84, 86: from the collection of the Metropolitan Life Insurance Company, NYC, photography by Malcolm Varon; p. 82: from the collection of the Bank of Boston; p. 94: photograph by William Ryerson, reprinted courtesy of *The Boston Globe* (reproduced courtesy of the Trustees of the Public Library of the City of Boston); p. 96: photograph by William Ryerson, reprinted courtesy of *The Boston Globe* (reproduced by permission of the Town of West Hartford); p. 105 bottom: photograph by William Ryerson, reprinted courtesy of *The Boston Globe* (reproduced by permission of the Ancient and Honorable Artillery Company of Massachusetts).

Color Well (Following page numbers refer to pages in color section.) Pp. 1 top, 2 top and bottom, 8 bottom: photographs by William Ryerson, reprinted courtesy of *The Boston Globe;* p. 1 bottom: photograph by William Ryerson, reprinted courtesy of *The Boston Globe* (reproduced by permission of St. Andrew's Church, Plymouth, England); p. 3 top: reprinted by permission of the Boston Athenaeum (color added); pp. 3 bottom, 4-5: from the collection of the Metropolitan Life Insurance Company, NYC, photography by Malcolm Varon; p. 6: photographs by William Ryerson, reprinted courtesy of *The Boston Globe* (reproduced by permission of the Pilgrim Hall Museum, Plymouth, Mass.); p. 7 top: photograph by William Ryerson, reprinted courtesy of *The Boston Globe* (reproduced by permission of the Pilgrim Monument & Provincetown Museum); p. 7 bottom (left and right): from the collection of the Bank of Boston; p. 8 top: photograph by William Ryerson, reprinted courtesy of *The Boston Globe* (reproduced by permission of the Commonwealth of Massachusetts, Massachusetts Archives at Columbia Point).

INDEX